The Wounded Healer

Find Your Health.
Discover Your Clarity.
Live Your Purpose.

Dr. Jason Mallia

BALBOA.
PRESS
A DIVISION OF HAY HOUSE

Balboa Press books may be ordered through booksellers or by contacting:

Balboa Press
A Division of Hay House
1663 Liberty Drive
Bloomington, IN 47403
www.balboapress.com.au
1 (877) 407-4847

Because of the dynamic nature of the Internet, any web addresses or links contained in this book may have changed since publication and may no longer be valid. The views expressed in this work are solely those of the author and do not necessarily reflect the views of the publisher, and the publisher hereby disclaims any responsibility for them.

The author of this book does not dispense medical advice or prescribe the use of any technique as a form of treatment for physical, emotional, or medical problems without the advice of a physician, either directly or indirectly. The intent of the author is only to offer information of a general nature to help you in your quest for emotional and spiritual well-being. In the event you use any of the information in this book for yourself, which is your constitutional right, the author and the publisher assume no responsibility for your actions.

Any people depicted in stock imagery provided by Thinkstock are models, and such images are being used for illustrative purposes only.
Certain stock imagery © Thinkstock.

ISBN: 978-1-5043-0490-0 (sc)
ISBN: 978-1-5043-0491-7 (e)

Print information available on the last page.

Balboa Press rev. date: 11/04/2016

Acknowledgements

First and foremost I would like to thank my parents, Joseph and Josephine, and my sister, Margaret, for their love and support, even when times were uncertain and the path for me was not always clear.

This book has been a labour of love and an evolutionary process over many years with its origins dating back to my early childhood and lessons learned through life's challenges, family, friends, and relationships. It is an honour and a privilege that I extend profound love and gratitude to those whom have taught, inspired, and helped me evolve into the person I am today. The book it dedicated to you. I would also like to acknowledge my teachers and masters whose wisdom has inspired me to be the healer I am today.

Immense gratitude to my love and life partner, Daniela, for being part of the journey and helping me serve my *telos*. Thank you for inspiring me to complete this book and for being my number-one fan. For that I will be forever grateful; I love you. A big thank you to the many patients and people whom I have been on a journey with during my clinical practice years as an Integrative Medicine Practitioner and Naturopath. You have been my teachers and my reason to get out of bed for many years. It is because of you I can now share my wisdom and knowledge to help the wider community of the world.

I would also like to thank you, the reader, for your support in reading this book and taking the responsibility to become the best human being you can be. Seeing people evolving and living happier, healthier lives with gratitude is my biggest reward and satisfaction.

Contributors

A big thank you to the following contributors. Without you this book would not be possible.

Peter Furst: first draft development

Daniela D'Aquino: co-editing

Jon-Michael Mooney: cover design

Contents

Introduction

"What Would it Have Been Like?"

What would it have been like before there was light?

A time of darkness and unconscious insight.

How would love have been without the confusion of words and the over intellect of which jades our path.

How would it have been in the summer and fall? Without man's aggression and intent of war.

How would the food taste, picked clean and ripe, would they have given us clarity, inspiration, and insight?

How would love be without the torment of the past? A love so pure with acceptance and joy.

A dance and connection for us to employ.

We are now here through our choices from past,

Our time is now to create a world evolved and ever-last.

Evolution is our lesson together, this is our creation.

Imagine a world of love motivation.

It would be like now, with a peace sensation.

—J. Mallia 1994

Part 1

Chapter 1

The Secret to Mastering Your Life

I am going to empower you to live a happy, healthy, and amazing life, the life you've always dreamt of.

There is a reason you are reading this book right now. Either consciously or subconsciously you have realised you need a tool to help you to live the life you want—abundant, happy, and fulfilling. You have been calling out for something to help you move forward in your life, to move you toward where you aspire to be, your true purpose. It is no coincidence that this book is in front of you. This book is a manifestation of something that you have created, something to help you live the life you've always dreamt of since you were a child. It is important to recognise and acknowledge that you are reading these words because it is something you have desired, and now you need to make the most of this information to create your destiny.

Give yourself a pat on the back for having brought this moment into existence. Congratulations on your first creation toward the life you want. It is important to believe this, as with this belief you will do it again and again for other things that you want throughout your life to come. You are the master creator and architect of your own life.

Obviously what we create for ourselves needs to be believable and realistic. We need to have a minimum of 80 percent belief that we can achieve whatever that goal may be, and with that belief we can bring it into our reality. You have demonstrated this now and by choosing to accept this, you can create the life you want. Health, longevity, vitality, happiness, and your life goals will be within your reach.

This book is a combination of many years of work and experience—as a healer, a practitioner, and a person. It aims to fast track your success, whereas it took me many years to develop these understandings through both study and life's challenges. I have condensed twenty years down into this book so that you can take this summarised information and utilise it. You do not have to spend a long time discovering the keys for yourself. You can harness the energy of my life and be fast tracked to success. By the end of this book you will have learned empowering tools to help you achieve what you want in this life. You will implement the tools to help you become the very best version of yourself and contribute to this world in the process. This will give you ultimate happiness and mastery of your life.

During my upheaval and growth, I learned many lessons. While some were difficult, I learned a lot from them and realised how awesome this was. I wanted to tell the whole world because I felt like it was my duty. That is where this book stems from. I am excited to pass on my lessons and knowledge. I want to help you change your life. When it comes to self-help, there is a lot of gimmicky information out there that people are being misled by. I want people to gain insight and truth, and I know this is true because I have lived it.

When I say, "One only heals when sense of self is recognised"—which you will read about later in part 2—it's not just a phrase, it's something I feel and have experienced. This is how I feel about everything that is written in this book. It has the truth of having been tested and lived through.

Perhaps you are reading this because you know or have realised there is something else out there for you. Perhaps your health isn't where you want it to be. Imagine being able to wake up every morning and feel like you are in control of your own happiness and destiny! Have you ever felt lost in life, been unhappy, not sure of what you want, or like your life is heading nowhere? Imagine living with clarity, having the ability to create your own life and happiness and knowing what you truly want. If you want to live to the full, experiencing life the way you should, then you need to have a plan. Throughout the course of this book, you will develop one.

My belief is that in order for us to be fulfilled we need to live a life of purpose, a life where we do what we're meant to be doing. The ancient Greeks called it *telos* and understood that we all have a purpose and dwell on this Earth to fulfil it. Self-help books are full of techniques for connecting you to achieving your telos, but my personal experience has reinforced to me that too often the role health plays is neglected or entirely overlooked. The focus on *health* is what sets this book apart.

If we are not healthy, then we lack the clarity of thought required to even know our telos. Without this foundation of good health we cannot enjoy lasting happiness. Too often people do not understand health. They think of it as just the absence of sickness and disease. Until we get sick, we don't even pay attention to being healthy. This is why most medicine focuses on treating symptoms rather than providing cures. True health, however, is a higher state of function where you feel alive and inspired. You have dreams. You are connected to other people. You are achieving your higher purpose, your telos.

People have been conditioned in the way they think about health. Most medical doctors will send patients away if the patients feel sick but test results don't show anything connected to an illness. As far as these doctors are concerned, you are healthy if your pathology tests are clear. This creates an environment of only recognising symptoms and diseases and not underlying health issues that could be developing. This results in only the symptoms and diseases being treated rather than promoting optimum health and wellness.

As long as the symptoms go away, people think they are healthy. At this point, this is when medical doctors should refer their patients to natural or integrative medical practitioners so they can improve their well-being rather than waiting around until they get unwell again. This is the problem. There is not enough direction given to people about preventive measures they can be taking to become the healthiest possible version of themselves. There is not enough emphasis on lifestyle and prevention. Instead, patients are only treated when there is recognisable evidence of a disease.

As a result, people do not seek getting better and becoming truly healthy. Instead, people just accept their status quo. They accept that they are getting older, that there is nothing better for them out there, they feel tired all the time as part of the stresses of life, and they put it down to age. We accept not being truly healthy as part of who we are because we do not realise how well we can really be. But it doesn't have to be that way. You can feel better by changing what you put into your body, how you think about your body, and what you do with your body.

Healing is a way of life; it's ongoing. Healing is about giving yourself the best possible platform from which to reach your maximum potential, from which to achieve your telos. We are all healing, and as a "healer," I am still healing. By reading this book, you are entering into a journey of healing along with me. Fortunately, your body is very responsive when you do what you are meant to do to help it.

I have profound confidence in the body's healing abilities, and you will too once you discover who you are and create the right environment for yourself—whether through the right diet, the right mind-set, the right exercise, or any combination of factors that you will learn about in these pages.

The key to allowing your body to heal itself is to put it in the right environment. Science has proven this, and one body of research by Dr. Bruce Lipton supports this. We once thought that we were at the mercy of our DNA; however, we have discovered otherwise. Scientists removed the DNA from functioning cells and observed their reaction to various environments. What they discovered was cells were not only being instructed by their DNA but by their environment. This explains why two people with very similar DNA such as twins can be different even though their DNA is the same. This is called epigenetics. This field of study acknowledges that cellular changes can occur due to lifestyle factors, such as diet and environment. Therefore, we are not controlled by our genes—we control them!

Your body already heals itself. You just need to listen to what it's crying out for and stop the barriers that are blocking its own ability to thrive, such as too much stress, the wrong diet, and environmental toxicity. These are the things that put the body under strain. They need to be reigned in to get the body back to a state of balance. Your body just needs to be shown the way.

The flipside of the body's healing abilities is that it can become defensive. If you do not create the right environment for your body, it is going to resist healing. For example, when you have a headache, your body is telling you something is wrong. If you just take painkillers, you're ignoring the signs of what your body is telling you. While it may control the pain in your body, it's not working in harmony with it. Many people get caught up in ignoring and suppressing symptoms without homing in on the root cause. The medical and pharmaceutical industries often focus on this too. Many medicines address symptoms and give people a sense of feeling better without truly healing them to a higher state of health. This approach can push the disease deeper until it eventually resurfaces with far worse consequences. It is too easy to get into a habit of regular symptomatic medication, but the body does not want to be suppressed—it wants to express its symptoms. Symptoms are actually a blessing. It is your body telling you something is wrong, giving you the opportunity to address it to change and grow.

Similarly, diseases are a gift from your body telling you that you are on the wrong path and need to get back on the right one. To be happy you need to be healthy, and that comes from creating the right environment, not just for healing but for reaching your ultimate potential.

We are all healing, whether it is from illness and disease or emotional and physical wounds. There are scars that are sometimes left behind, but those scars shape who we are if we choose to move toward what we want. Fortunately, the body is resilient and is meant to evolve through these challenges. We move through stagnation into change and growth.

In fact, many people who have been sick report that their illness is a blessing and that they move toward what they truly want in the process, facilitating connectedness to themselves and a deeper sense of love and care for others.

Healing is actually a spiritual experience because you have to rise above your pain and situation. The pain and suffering are trying to push you down, but if you develop resilience and understanding of why you have gotten sick, then you do not have to fear being unwell but instead view it as a lesson. It forces a change upon you, whether it be in your diet, lifestyle, job, or relationship. Your body tells you that something is not right. Illness is a representation of the change that needs to happen. It is a gift.

However, if we choose to self-medicate and numb our pain, then the spiritual lessons will not be learned and we will not evolve.

When you are not living, you are dying. If you are not present in your life and clear and appreciative of what you are living among, you are not really living. There is the state of being alive and then there is truly living. When people experience an illness, they can actually become more alive.

Diseases often make people think deeply about their lives. When they recover, they realise they've been given another chance. They are determined to make the most of their lives and not waste them. They do not take things for granted. When I went through my various injuries and diseases, I knew they were setting me up for my purpose.

Rather than waiting for symptoms or disease to strike and take you to a medical clinic, I will show you how to become proactive about living a healthy life. You have the ability to change how you heal and how you feel just by understanding yourself and being in tune with your body. The key to natural medicine is in encouraging your body's own healing processes to flow.

There will always be a need to occasionally seek assistance from medical doctors and pharmaceuticals, but the rest of the time the responsibility for our health is with ourselves. Fortunately, my life has taught me that it is often possible to heal myself. After sharing my story, I will teach you how to work with your body and mind to help you realise your own healing potential.

My education into natural medicine was born through misfortune and hard work. I was always a sceptic, and no doubt many of you are too, but time and time again I have been shown the value of the path we are now both walking. This path not only gives us healthy bodies but connects us to our ultimate goals in life.

In order to empower you to master your life, this book will teach you to become your own healer and guide you through establishing a plan that will improve your health and connect you with achieving your telos.

The Five Human Elements of Life Mastery

Along with ancient philosophers, many modern-day philosophers agree that to achieve happiness, we must live to our full potential. There are five main elements to achieve this. I like to refer to them as the five human elements of life mastery:

- Connected to your telos
- Connected to values and esteem needs
- Love, relationships and social interaction
- Security and stability needs
- Physical, emotional, mental health essentials

Underpinning the five elements is our requirement of optimum health on all levels. Health is the main focus of this book. Optimum health will give you clarity, enabling you to make the right choices in alignment with your overall purpose in life.

Diagram A

The Five Human Elements of Life Mastery

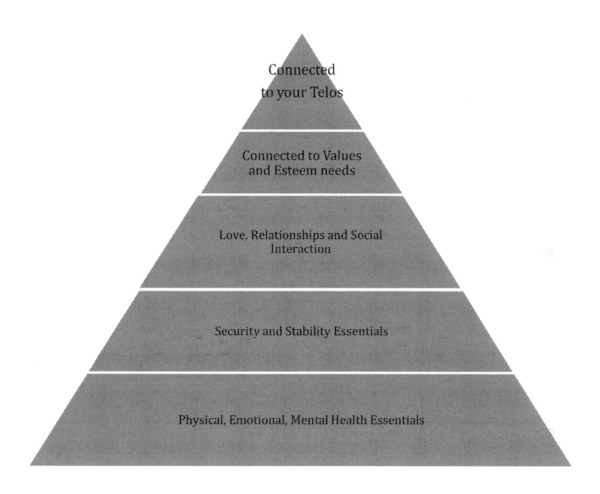

Chapter 2

The Journey of the Wounded Healer

Understanding why health is the foundation of a happy and fulfilling life has been the result of nearly two decades of personal experience backed by academic study and dealing with illnesses and diseases of patients in my Integrative Medicine and Naturopathic clinical practice. This was the answer to a question I never even planned on asking.

As a child I lived for rugby league. It was my life. It was everything. It was the only thing I knew and loved apart from my family. Football gave me an opportunity to spend time with friends, to release my energy, and to release my emotions. Every morning when I woke up, I thought about football. Every night when I went to sleep, I dreamed about football.

It was that way from the first moment I started playing as a child. When I was five or six years old I was waiting for my father to take me to training, but we stopped at my grandmother's place first. I was so frustrated and annoyed that we had gone there first instead of going straight to training. I desperately wanted to go to training, but they were holding me back. I waited in the car while they went inside, and I told them to hurry because I didn't want to be late.

They took far too long, and I was becoming more frustrated and impatient. So I jumped in the driver's seat and tried to drive myself to training. Obviously, I didn't know what I was doing. I put the car in gear but it started rolling backward. It was out of control! The car went through an empty intersection and crashed into a house. An old man usually sat on the porch every day, but that day he miraculously wasn't there. The car went straight through the porch and into the front bedroom of his fibro house in Balmain. I had even hit a pole that snapped in half and somehow ended up smashing through the back window of the car, almost decapitating me.

I couldn't believe no one was injured. Thankfully, the pole missed my head. All I really wanted at that moment was to go to football training!

When the police arrived, I was quick-thinking enough to tell the officer that while jumping from the backseat to the front of the car I had accidentally hit the gear stick and when the car started moving I didn't know what to do. That wasn't true, but I was worried that my dad would get in trouble. Fortunately, the officer knew I was just a kid doing a silly thing, so he turned a blind eye to it.

For me, football was the best thing that ever happened because it enabled me to make friends and be accepted. Since I was very good at it, I was welcomed and respected by my peers.

I remember watching the high school competition on television, which was then called the Commonwealth Bank Cup. I was determined to be there when I was old enough. As the years passed my skills developed, and I achieved that ultimate dream and my first dream creation moment. I played on television several times and even took the field with the likes of game greats Brad Fittler, Jason Taylor, and Jacin Sinclair. My dream had come true, so I then strived to achieve an even bigger dream, which was to play on Leichhardt oval with the Tigers first grade team. However, after years of intense training, my dream was sadly crushed.

The Tigers didn't choose me when I completed my studies at Holy Cross College High School. I was extremely hurt, angry, and devastated. I strongly believed they should have recruited me because I was good enough, but back then I thought there were a lot of politics involved. Players who seemed to know someone in authority were being chosen instead of more talented players. Also, the game was evolving, and the type of player they were looking for was changing. I was an old-school footballer, more in the style of hard-hitting Australian representative David Gillespie or fellow Kangaroo forward Steve Folkes. During that time they had started to recruit taller and faster players.

Despite my first grade dream fading, I still loved football and played for a Tigers feeder team. I was twenty-one and playing the best I ever had. I was also enjoying myself off the field going out drinking and partying with my mates. This was the time of flat top hairstyles, singing duo Milli Vanilli, and singer Bobby Brown. I used to go out clubbing on the weekend wearing my track pants.

My dad was putting the hard word on me by telling me that if I wasn't going to make money with rugby league, then I shouldn't bother playing. This created self-doubt and my belief faded. He questioned my dedication and my drinking and said it wasn't worth the risk of injuries, but I loved the game so much. I loved playing with my mates. During that time I thought I had a great life—chicks, clubbing, mates, drinking—but my soul was asking underlying questions.

One dull foggy morning ensured rugby league would play no bigger part in my life any longer. The field was cold and eerie. I could smell the fresh-cut grass. My friends watched on from the grandstand. I was playing the best football of my career and riding high. The game was travelling well. I'd gone up with the line and completed a clean first-up tackle. I got back on side and pulled off another crisp hit. Going for a third, my worst nightmare occurred, something I never imagined would happen to me. My right leg snapped from under me! I'd never been injured in my life, but now it seemed that time stood still. I screamed in excruciating pain!

My lower leg was facing the other way around. I had broken the fibula and dislocated my ankle. The trainer ran on the field with a horrified look on his face. Within the next ten or fifteen minutes an ambulance was on the field, and I was now wearing an oxygen mask and being rushed to hospital. They put me on laughing gas, so I went from screaming in pain to laughing in the ambulance. The next thing I knew I was in hospital and a lovely nurse was jabbing me with morphine. The pain wasn't bad once the drugs kicked in. They performed emergency surgery on me that night, fusing my leg together with plates and pins. I spent an agonising week in hospital. It felt like my footballing dreams were over! However, I didn't realise that it was also the beginning of something else. In an instant, my life's path had changed.

As soon as that tackle occurred, everything in my life suddenly shifted. While I was in the hospital, my mates were going out drinking and I was left there feeling sorry for myself.

After I was discharged, I would go out with them, but while they were enjoying themselves, I could sense that everyone was feeling sorry for me. I had never had an injury in my life before, but this one freak injury ended my dream.

I used to say I would make a comeback, but I knew deep down inside that I would never want to go through that pain again. The doctor told me blankly, "No, you won't play football again. It's too risky." I believed him as I thought a doctor should know best about these things.

Three months later I had the plates removed and the doctor said I should be able to walk straight after the operation. Instead, I collapsed to the ground! I was fresh out of the operation, so I figured I would just have to give the wound time to heal.

A couple of weeks later I began to feel pain in my leg. I knew something wasn't right. The wound wasn't healing. I went back to the hospital and found out an infection had developed. They put me on a heavy antibiotic drip. The nurses had to squeeze the puss out of the wound, and then it was cleaned and stitched up.

It should have finally been healing properly, but once again I was soon in pain, and this time it was excruciating. I went back to see the surgeon, but he dismissed me, saying there was nothing wrong with me.

Fortunately, my old football trainer for the Holy Cross team was also a doctor, so I went to see him. If I trusted anyone with my health, it was him. He took one look at my leg, touched it with his hand, and knew it had developed into a bone infection. I got scans that proved him right. I needed heavy antibiotics for one whole year to try to rid my body of the infection.

After six months there was no improvement, and I feared the worst. If they couldn't cure the infection, they would need to amputate my leg. I was terrified! Since toddlerhood, running around had been a fundamental part of my life, and now I was facing the prospect of never doing it again. Making it worse, I felt no one understood what I was going through. I was alone and being dragged through fear and uncertainty.

For one painfully long year this torment continued. I tried to ignore my fears, but it wasn't until twelve agonising months later that I finally had the relief of receiving an all-clear. I'd never felt more relieved in my whole life. It was more than dodging a bullet. I felt like my life had been restored. I had been given another chance.

At this point I had lost faith in the medical profession, except for my old trainer. Even though he had saved my leg, I was disillusioned with the whole profession. Highlighting my frustration, rugby league great Ricky Stuart suffered the same injury the same weekend as me and recovered within three months. I was looking at him getting better, and I was experiencing all these problems. While I was getting my plates taken out, he was back on the field playing.

During this year I struggled with depression, and the heavy medication had taken its toll. Knowing that my dream was over, I turned to more drinking and drugs to numb my pain. I was spiralling downhill fast. Somewhere in the darkness of my despair I hit a breaking point, and something shifted. I started questioning what I should do with my life because I knew this wasn't the answer.

I was a good lateral thinker and decided to focus on rising out of my depression. I made a decision to start training again. I started eating well and began to do restorative things for my body instead of destructive ones, such as eating a healthy diet, cutting out alcohol and drugs, and exercising more. At that time, this event made me feel like it was the worst thing in the world, but now when I look back, it is actually what has shaped me into who I am today. Eventually, the infection healed and it felt like a big weight had been lifted, and I could finally get on with my life.

I did some more research and started eating properly. Diet was already helping me with my physique and my rehabilitation, and I became stronger and fitter than ever before.

Knowing my rugby league career was over, I thought I should start using my brain. I had been using my brawn all my life, playing football and not listening in school, but then I made a decision to step up to the plate and begin using my intellect.

One day I was in a health food shop and asked the guy working there what he did for a living, and he said he was a naturopath. A natural medicine doctor that helped people heal using natural remedies. I just looked at him with a puzzled look on my face until he explained. I asked him where I could learn about nutrition, so he gave me the details of a college. I rang them the very same day and booked into a nutrition course, thinking I was just interested in doing it for my own benefit and knowledge. I was only interested in how I was going to fix my own body. I wasn't thinking about anything else or any bigger picture just yet.

The course was very interesting, and to my surprise I started achieving outstanding grades. I thought I was just a dumb football jock. I appeared dumb because I played in the front row and didn't have the best English skills. When I studied nutrition, I realised I wasn't bad at it. I surprised myself because I was achieving results in the highest percentile of the class. I wasn't that dumb after all and realised I hadn't been giving myself the credit I deserved. It was the first bit of study I had done since school. I was a football jock and hadn't been interested in school at all, but I was certainly interested in this. It wasn't until two years into my studies that I found out it was a professional course that would qualify me as a nutritionist!

While I was seemingly on a path to clean living, I also had a history of being a party boy. I had been prescribed steroids in a last-ditch attempt to make it back as a rugby league player. I got built up and was looking fantastic. I was going out clubbing all hours of the night. I was at a peak physically, but mentally I wasn't right. I thought I was happy because I was looking good and had the girlfriend that everybody wanted. We were the "it" couple. Everyone loved us and wanted to be around us. I think it was all an illusion because in hindsight, I wonder if I would have been that happy if I wasn't going out and having party drugs and dope every second day. I was living a hypocritical life. On one hand, I was trying to fix my body and strengthen it, but at the same time I was damaging it. It was like a tug of war between the old version of myself and the best version of myself.

After two years of studying nutrition, I thought I would take a break to decide if I really wanted to pursue it, so I decided to travel the world, soul searching. Prior to leaving home, I had broken up with my girlfriend. She was great but was a party girl who wanted to keep partying, and I was trying to break free from that environment. It was time for me to get serious about my life and to lay a foundation for my health and career. She chose partying over moving forward with me. I chose to move forward to study, grow, and heal. It broke my heart, but I had to move on. It was very difficult because she was my best friend. We were together all the time. It was a big heartbreak.

I lived and worked in the Maltese Islands and travelled around Europe, all the time reflecting on my life back home. Always looking into the picture of my life in Australia from abroad, however, and by the end of the year I realised I was wasting my time in Malta. I had much to offer the world, and the environment I was in was limiting my opportunities as it was such a small island.

One day while working in a gym, our resident physiotherapist called in sick. The boss came to me and said, "Jason, you'll be doing the massages today."

Confused and overwhelmed, I explained that I wasn't a qualified massage therapist and that I had never even touched a body before except in a personal training session.

His response was, "How hard could it be? You know the anatomy of the body. Just massage the muscles and use your common sense."

So ignoring my fear of the unknown, I took a leap of faith. Being in Europe, my first client was a middle-aged German woman who walked in naked (I later found out that this was normal for some parts of Europe). After getting over the initial shock, I started massaging and performed a few sport stretches on her. The client seemed to benefit from the treatment. Interestingly, to my surprise I seemed to know exactly what to do as soon as I put my hands on the client—my hands just knew where to go. My instincts kicked in, and that was the moment I learned two things. One, I had to leave the gym and get back to Australia to keep studying natural medicine and to further develop my massage skills. Secondly, and most importantly, I had learned to push through fear and to trust the flow of life as you never know where it might lead and that growth is the ultimate reward of pushing through your fears.

Armed with these new lessons, I had a newfound belief that I had a lot to offer the world and this was being wasted working one-on-one in my current job. It felt like there was something bigger and better coming my way. It was another breakthrough.

I had also come to the realisation that what I went to do in Malta—to reflect on my life and recharge, reconnect, and redirect, and most importantly to heal—had been accomplished. I told myself I had to get inspired again. I had to embrace the opportunities calling me, so I returned home to Sydney.

Despite my intentions and new goals, turning my life around was a slow process. I was still battling old demons while trying to move in the right direction. One evening while in a seedy nightclub doing things I shouldn't have been doing, a notorious figure who knew my family walked up to me. I was excited to see him as he had always been like a father figure to me, but surprisingly he didn't seem to share the same excitement to see me.

He said, "What are you doing here? What are you doing with your life? You come from a good family, Jas—get out of this place. It's not for you!"

Here was someone I respected giving me a straight-out blunt warning! I didn't know anything about what he did. I just saw him as a decent human being. He knew there was something better out there for me. He knew I was a good kid at heart.

In that moment it felt like time stood still. A feeling of anxiety overwhelmed my body. I immediately left the club, and on my way home, my internal dialogue said, *He's right. I do come from a good family. What am I doing? I need to clean up my act.* When someone like that tells you to clean up your act, it carries quite a lot of weight.

I talked to my parents and admitted what I'd been doing. I was ashamed but announced it so they knew I was committed to changing my life for the better and could hold me accountable. They were relieved because they knew something was going on, but I was honest with them, and they knew it was the end of my dark days. They knew a major time for change and growth was in store for me.

My parents are interesting people because they always like to think the best. They trusted that I knew what I was doing. They always knew I was self-sufficient, and they stayed out of my way. Of course, they would try to influence me, but they knew I was always going to learn life's lessons my own way—the hard way—no matter what they told me. I was one of those kids that you couldn't tell too much to. Fortunately, I've always had a good family to fall back on.

That one moment in the club had really made me stop and think about my life. I then listened to my intuition and followed a more fulfilling path. There were so many situations that I was getting pulled into. Every time I tried to walk away, it was like negative forces and negative people pulled me back in. I had to dissociate, break free, and start creating a whole new clean life for myself. From that point I turned a corner. I didn't want to continue down the dark path I'd been on.

This was another crucial moment that pushed me toward turning my life around. Until then I had thought that breaking my leg was, but that was a forced change. It didn't really wake me up to what I was doing. Drinking and drugs had kept me in a trance. That moment in the club really woke me up. It was a pivotal point and when I began to move forward and leave everything negative behind.

Despite the naysayers, this led me to focus on my new path. I began changing my environment. I started cleaning up my act, I became open to learn and grow, and my life began to change.

However, despite that moment in that seedy nightclub, something fiercely dark pulled me back in again. Drugs ironically put me on the right path once again later in my life. One night I was feeling a little depressed and in need to go out and let off steam. Studying for years had left me feeling isolated and in a transitory period between old friends and new. You could say I was feeling lonely and misunderstood. Going down the nightclub path felt immensely wrong, but I chose to ignore that feeling. I felt a battle within me between my former self and my latter self. My dark side wanted to take an ecstasy pill to have fun again even though my light side knew it was going in the wrong direction for my life. The dark side took hold of me and won that night.

When I took the pill, I thought of it as a final farewell to my old self. I thought that I needed it as final closure to that part of the life. Unfortunately, that triggered a massive psychotic episode. I hadn't taken any drugs in eight years, not even a Panadol, but it was New Year's Eve and I thought it would be the last time and that I would be fine. Instead, it hit me like a tonne of bricks. A huge sense of anxiety overwhelmed my body. I became psychotic, irrational, and suicidal. It was terrifying! I even rang my parents and told them I loved them. I never said that sort of stuff. They immediately knew something was wrong. I felt like someone was chasing me. I was going through this fear of death. I felt like people were after me and that people in the streets were looking strangely at me. Filled with paranoia, I started roaming and running through the streets, not knowing where to turn. In that moment of complete and utter despair, I reached out for help.

Having grown up as a Catholic, I said, "God, if you help me right now, I promise to serve a purpose of good, change my ways, and be of service to others, and if you're out there, I need your help right now!"

Within seconds of asking, help miraculously arrived! My cousin turned up in his car. I don't know how he knew where I was or how he found out what happened, but he took me home. He got me to a safe place. When I walked in the door, my parents were beside themselves with worry. I had scared them into thinking something bad had happened to me.

The next morning when I woke up, I thought I would be able to shrug it off, but I couldn't. I thought it would be like any other hangover, but this time was intensely different. I felt a weight on my spirit, a strange haze that was clouding my body, mind, and soul. The paranoia had remained. For a couple of weeks, whenever I saw certain people in suits or sitting in cars, I thought they were from the CIA and that they were watching me and I was being followed.

After a couple of weeks of this torment, I knew something had to shift. I made an appointment with a lady who worked as a psychic healer next door to me in Leichhardt.

As soon as I walked in, she said, "Jason, what have you been doing?" She looked behind my eyes and said I had something attached to me. She was a healer and an exorcist and said a demon had possessed me.

This was one of the most profound experiences I have ever had. I walked in one way and walked out a completely new person. She told me I was a healer and that demons attach to healers because they want to take them away from doing healing work. I remember thinking it was pretty far-fetched, but what she did worked.

Imagine a haze in your head, playing with your mind and causing a feeling of anxiety in your body. By the time I walked out, it was completely lifted. That was the absolute final event that pushed me away from pharmaceuticals and any kind of drug intervention or chemical influence. That was the final time I touched any sort of drug. She made it clear that those things don't suit me and that I had important work to do in this life as a healer. While it was a life-threatening moment and a time of profound upheaval, the events that transpired again guided me back on the right path that I had subconsciously chosen when enrolling into nutrition a decade earlier, that of a healer.

Even when I wasn't trying to find my purpose, it seemed my purpose was trying to find me. Looking back, I realise my purpose has always been drawing me to itself, from when I injured my leg to being confronted by my family friend to this moment when it struck home harder than at any other time in my life. I knew I had to turn my life around and live according to my purpose. I knew some higher power was pulling the strings and that something greater is out there.

I have always believed that there is a God because whenever I have asked for help, as I did in that drug situation, it has been provided. I have been in situations where I have asked God or the universe for a sign and have immediately received one. When I have followed the sign, the situation has turned out well, but at other times I haven't listened and ended up in a bad place.

What the psychic healer did for me was restore my faith and reconnect me to my higher self, to my light. As a healer, I am not really the one who does the work. I am a facilitator. You come to me and I connect you to what you need. You might come into my clinic and I know right away what therapy you need. It just comes to me. This stems from my education, but I also believe that a lot comes from intuition from a higher source. I feel I am guided.

I'm also one of those people who carries good energy. Sometimes I'm able to help someone heal by just doing the bare minimum. It's humbling that my patients are able to heal the way they do. It's a natural gift that has been given to me, and during the process of healing myself, I grew in confidence of my abilities and the medicine that I practice. I have good instincts and often know what is right for a person.

One of my first jobs as a nutritionist was as a contractor for the Tigers football players, the team I had once hoped to play for. They gave me an opportunity to work in player development. Part of the job was to deliver talks on nutrition to the team. I remember player Beau Ryan being a smart arse in the crowd and heckling me: "Are you nervous or something?" I was speaking to a group for the first time.

As I started to practice nutrition with the Tigers, I questioned whether they appreciated it. I decided I would rather work with the general public, who probably need it more than sports people who already think they know everything. Sports people are often only interested in performance and not necessarily interested in health. I spoke to them about needing good health to be able to perform well, and they all looked at me like I was an alien. You can have fitness without health, but true fitness is when you are healthy underneath. If you don't recover and your immune system doesn't recover, you're not going to consistently perform on the field. You're going to get injured. I was trying to preach that, but they weren't listening.

Whilst I was working with the Tigers, I also worked in private practice. My first clinical case was an old lady with osteoporosis. I was so passionate about nutrition that I was confident I could help her heal. It took nearly two years of treatment, but I helped her halt the progression of her osteoporosis. It was my first major success, which inspired me to know more and to start looking for other treatments. That to me was my calling. I knew I could do it. I wanted to treat people with chronic diseases. I had turned my back on sports nutrition and working for sports clubs. They only wanted to punish their bodies, not really heal them. I was more interested in seeing people heal and move forward.

At the end of my nutritional studies my college dean suggested I would make a good naturopath. I thought of those people as just a bunch of leaf-eating weirdos and hippies.

But in actual fact, I discovered that a naturopath is a scientifically trained doctor of natural medicine who helps patients heal their ailments using natural medicine, rather than surgery and pharmaceuticals. Despite this, I had experimented with taking herbs and noticed they worked for me. I was seeing what they could do and thought I should study herbal medicine. Soon I was hooked and on my way to becoming a naturopath.

It took twelve years to become a fully fledged naturopath—you need to pass five diplomas: nutritional medicine, herbal medicine, homeopathic medicine, remedial massage, and iridology. I never stopped questioning how strong this medicine was, but it always provided the answer. While I was working as a nutritionist and an herbalist in Bondi, I was struck down with mercury poisoning. One day while driving home from the clinic, my nose started bleeding. I felt anxious and agitated. As I glanced toward the backseat I noticed the blood pressure device in my bag was broken. I later discovered that the mercury inside the device had vaporised. It was a hot day, and without realising, I had been inhaling mercury vapours while driving. I soon realised I had been inhaling them all day since I had dropped my bag and broken the device while being at work. I became intoxicated.

I knew mercury poisoning was also known as mad hatter's disease, and sure enough, it made me a little nuts. I was paranoid and did a lot of research on it. I took six months off work. I lost nearly fifteen kilograms as the mercury got inside my system and sped it up. My heart was pumping out of my chest, and my thyroid was acting like I was on speed. I felt like a frail ninety-year-old woman. My bodybuilder's physique turned skinny in a short space of time. Everyone wondered what was wrong with me.

I turned to natural medicine for a solution. I visited an herbalist colleague who put me on the right program. It helped immensely and in the process strengthened my faith in the profession. The sickness also introduced me to the power of homeopathy. Homeopathy is the system of complementary medicine in which ailments are treated by minute doses of natural substances that in larger amounts would produce symptoms of the ailment. Previously I had always slagged off homeopathy, thinking it was nonsense and its practitioners were all weird. Surely that medicine could not work.

Despite my doubts I took the homeopathic medicine, and just one dose cleared everything out of my system and set me on the path to recovery. Mind you, it still took six months to start feeling like I could function and a couple of years before I cleared it completely out of my system.

Suffering from mercury poisoning wasn't the only time that my body questioned the validity of natural medicine. When I questioned it, the medicine spoke for itself. After studying homeopathy, I went heavily into practice as a naturopath. I was treating a lot of people and still doing a lot of massage work when I was struck down with chronic fatigue syndrome. I literally couldn't get out of bed, but with the help of some practitioners, I was able to heal myself in a very short space of time. Some of my patients can take up to four years to get right. Within three months I was up and flying due to my strong determination, mind-set and the ability to pinpoint the underlying cause of my illness.

Even with the success of treating my mercury poisoning and chronic fatigue, I became disillusioned with naturopathy again. I'm a massive sceptic and kept becoming disillusioned. It takes a lot to convince me of something. The only thing I wasn't sceptical about was nutrition. I had seen that healthy food made me feel better. I was still sceptical about herbs and homeopathy.

I began working as a naturopath within some chiropractic clinics and discovered the benefits that it could achieve through correcting spinal misalignments. I thought I should study to become a chiropractor as well, so I completed my bachelor's degree. With this knowledge under my belt I realised I didn't want to focus on just one discipline but wanted to be more of an integrative practitioner.

Through my time as a practitioner and through my own healing, I had realised how important it was to integrate treatments. In my first clinic I had a chiropractor, a naturopath, a homeopath, a massage therapist, and a nurse practitioner. It was one of the first integrative health clinics in Australia. Unfortunately, I found it difficult to integrate the treatments because everyone had their own ideas, and there are a lot of egos involved in natural medicine: every person thought his or her system was better than the others. All I was concerned with was finding the best system for the patient.

It was not working, so I realised I was better off studying as much as I could to become the best integrative practitioner I could be. After studying chiropractic medicine, I went on to study acupuncture and am now a registered Chinese medicine practitioner.

Before studying it, I thought acupuncture was a bit weird. In a clinic I had worked in, a practitioner used to question me about my naturopathy. She never really bought the Western approach and started educating me about her type of medicine. I had treatments with her and always felt good afterward. This remains one of my favourite aspects of the treatment I provide. Acupuncture provided a major string to my bow. It added another dimension to what I was doing and rounded off my knowledge.

Finally, I completed my studies with a pair of doctorate degrees on integrative medicine in the United States. A lot of naturopaths and doctors in the states do postgraduate studies on natural medicine to integrate both sides of the spectrum. With my formal education complete, I now focused on bringing it all together and educating and inspiring others. I wanted to save people from having to endure my nearly two decades of study, clinical practice, and dealing with illness and disease to fast track them into getting results.

I don't see myself now as only a naturopath because they are seen as alternative practitioners. I don't see myself as alternative. I see myself as *integrative.* There's a difference. I use a lot of medical tests and I work a lot with medical doctors. In the process of becoming integrative, I learned the medical model. I advise that everyone see their doctor first and then consult with a natural medicine practitioner. I have learned a lot about medicine through my own experience, through other people's experiences, and through the testing that they have had done. I have learned how to look from both sides and to integrate this understanding for the patients to generate the best results for them.

Every modality that I have ever studied and adopted happened because I had felt there was something lacking in my repertoire. I got to a point with my first patient, the one with osteoporosis, where I realised there was only so much I could do with just nutritional medicine. I needed to bring something else to her treatment, so I turned to herbal medicine. We integrated those treatments along with mainstream treatment.

As I then started to see different kinds of patients, I was treating complex conditions that needed a repertoire of skills—some people needed pain medicines, some needed physical treatments, some needed internal medicine, some needed nutrition, and some needed counselling. To address my patients' needs, I kept adding to my skills. I became a naturopath because they are skilled in most disciplines—physiological, mental, emotional, and structural.

I expanded my skill set further by studying chiropractic. I studied acupuncture. I sought out integrative medicine. I learned about blood testing. I learned injection therapy. I learned whatever was needed when I came across a difficult patient. This study process has gotten me to a point where I now feel well rounded. I am now positioned to be a good judge of what is the best direction for a person.

The overriding legacy from my years of education and practice is that I developed confidence in my healing ability of the body. When the environment is right, healing takes place. This was reinforced at each step.

Everything I learned was a result of something happening in my life. That is what gave me the passion to learn more and the confidence in what I had learned. I know that there are a lot of sceptics of natural medicine, and that is why you've got to experience it first-hand. I have met a lot of sceptics and I was one too, but it's always interesting to see the change in them when they or someone they care for benefit from it.

Scepticism is healthy. You might be sceptical as you read these pages. What I challenge you to do is to put it to the test. Read what is on offer in this book, and do your own research, but most importantly, take steps to put your body in the right environment for it to be able to heal itself. If anything gets you into that space of feeling better, then that's a win. You have to be brave and you need a little bit of blind faith at first, but once you see some results, you will share my confidence.

Throughout my journey as a wounded healer, natural medicine has enabled me to heal myself and others, and now I want to teach others how to heal themselves. As I will continue to reinforce this, being truly healthy is crucial to connecting you with achieving your telos, and only this will give you lasting happiness.

Chapter 3

Reaching your Potential

Now that you know why I am so inspired by natural medicine, it is time to ask yourself if you are ready to be inspired too. Are you happy with the status quo? Do you want a better life for yourself? The way you feel can inspire you to achieve everything you want in life. How you feel ultimately dictates what you're able to achieve in this world. Take a moment and ask yourself: What do I want for my life? How much do I want it? Why am I here? How do I want to live my life? What do I choose now? What lies between me and my success?

At some point, many people come to a crossroads where they are faced with a choice. Your existence today is a result of a series of choices and decisions made, from the person you chose as your partner to your food choices. Everything we are is connected to our choices. In order to be fulfilled in life, you need to make the choices that are in alignment with your overall purpose, your telos. It's what you truly want to achieve in this life; your ultimate reason for being here.

Part of my telos is to travel the world inspiring, educating, and helping people live their true potential—to get as many people involved in the process of healing and evolving, ultimately taking us back to our true innate selves living in peace and harmony with the planet and one another.

When asking the above big questions of your life to find your telos, it is essential to listen to your heart. Too often, self-help books just talk about mind-set and not enough about the heart and its connection to the mind. That is why health is so easily overlooked with these approaches and ultimately why they can fail to have a lasting impact in people's lives.

In traditional Chinese medicine, it has long been known that the heart is the house of the mind—meaning there is a brain inside the heart. This may seem like a strange concept to those who have just been brought up with mainstream Western medicine. Eastern and Western medicine agree that a healthy heart is crucial for a healthy life, due to the heart's role in circulating blood throughout the body, but in Chinese medicine, it is recognised that the heart also regulates aspects of health such as sleep, clarity, memory, and emotional well-being.

The link has been proven more recently. The heart has been scientifically shown to have cells that act like brain cells and navigate us through life. Neurologist Dr. Andrew Amour of Montreal discovered the heart contains a sophisticated set of neurons, called sensory neurites, that are organised in its own nervous system and directly communicate with the brain. The mind is really the body's computer. The heart is what you need to follow. If you follow your heart and the connection between the heart and the brain is sound due to good health, you will end up where you need to be. You will find your true calling.

Natural medicine provides tools that you can use to achieve your purpose. It helps you feel more balanced and more at ease. Any healing art helps you to heal, and if you heal you are going to feel more connected to your higher purpose.

Living an amazing happy and healthy life seems like something we should embrace without a second thought, but most people experience a resistance to taking the necessary steps to getting better. Those who resist choose to not exist how they were meant to live. Many people are confronted with a resistance to change, as I have at various stages of my life. There is often a block; we may fear the unknown, and because we don't really understand what healing is, we delay the process.

We've been conditioned to think about healing only in terms of addressing symptoms. If we don't have any symptoms, then we don't do anything to heal ourselves. If you're feeling that way now, you're not alone. What is important is to take the first steps. Once you start to feel the benefits of becoming truly healthy, resistance will quickly disappear.

With the knowledge you will receive, you will never be the same again. People don't realise this until they start to feel good, and once this happens these new states become anchored in your memory, providing a reference point for a higher state of function, should you wish to grow further. Remember, if you're not growing, you're dying, so nourish yourself and to keep growing in all areas.

It almost becomes addictive when you feel it the first time. There was a period in my life when I didn't feel well for years. Knowing something wasn't right at various stages in my own development, I chose to take control of my health and develop further toward mastering my health and ultimately becoming the teacher I am today.

When you start to function on a higher level, the only questions that remain are: How much better can I be? How much more can I learn? How much more can I grow? What else is out there for me?

As we evolve as human beings, whether it be in our health or in our lives, it is a process. The four main levels of learning and growth start from an unconscious-incompetent level and proceeds to an unconscious automatic competence level. The end state is where we have attained enough growth to make what we learn an unconscious automatic action. Many people stop here and wonder why all of a sudden life feels monotonous or they have stopped being happy or are lacking fulfilment. So I have added an extra two stages: mastery and enlightenment, to help people understand further progression if they choose to develop further.

If we choose to go beyond the four main stages to include mastery, teaching, and inspiring others, it becomes possible if this is our calling. If we decide mastery is not for us, we may choose to change our focus toward a different challenge and start the process again.

Diagram B

The Six Stages to Growth and Enlightenment

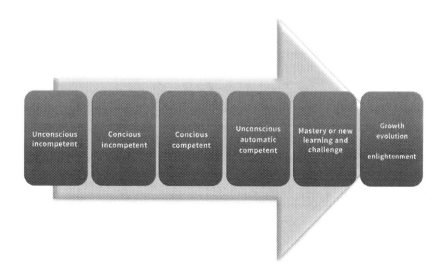

This book aims to elevate you through the stages from unconscious incompetent to being automatically unconscious-competent in your seven-step program. Should you wish to move to the higher (added) levels, further development will be required beyond this book. The program will help you understand which level you're on the continuum in each area of your health and life. At the automatically competent state, you will be plugged in and switched on and inspiring people automatically by your actions, having achieved a new level of health and energy. You intentionally decide how to live your life, and from this new level, you develop further skills to live in alignment with your telos and ultimately harness this energy to help others.

In the growth and learning process, the majority of people begin in a state of unconscious incompetency in whatever they're attempting to grow through. Let's use driving a car as an example. Let's say you decide you want to drive and have no license. You start with no skills to begin with and are not aware of what to do. This is the stage of unconscious incompetence. You then take a written test, which increases your knowledge and awareness, but at this stage you still need the physical skills to drive. You pass the test and are now in a mode of conscious incompetence. The next stage is for you to learn with an instructor, and this develops your driving skills. So now you have skills, and this moves you into a new mode of conscious competency, a mode where you still have to be conscious of what you're doing while driving a car. As you drive more and more and your skills increase, they become automatic, and you move into a mode called unconscious or automatic competency, where you can drive without having to focus on the minor details. At this stage you become automatically controlled by your unconscious mind, allowing for consciousness of other sensory information such as the music on the radio or taking in scenery as you drive.

Let's say you're now automatic in your driving skills and want to develop further and reach a higher level. You may choose to learn to master driving and become a race car driver or a driving instructor. In order for you to achieve mastery, further skills development will be required by a master teacher to help you evolve. If you choose not to develop further and accept your level, you may focus on developing another area of your life. You are in the driver's seat!

Similar to driving a vehicle, you are in the driver seat of your own health and life. As we develop, it is our choices that ultimately decide what turns we take and whether we choose to move toward mastery, growth, and enlightenment.

Let's now take a look at it from a global consciousness angle. Globally what I see is that many people live day to day unconsciously competent. Having accepted this level of existence, while this may keep people on the payroll and in a job, it starts to become monotonous and uninspiring, almost robotic. It is at this time they either feel unwell and their bodies begin to show signs of stagnation. If you take a look around, most people are competent enough to be able do everything from driving a car to working as lawyers or doctors, but they are often living an uninspired life. They fail to get their hearts involved in what they're doing. Things happen to them rather than being done by them. One can only imagine what they could achieve if they became inspired. Imagine what you could achieve with more heartfelt clarity and more inspiration.

What snapped me out of my unconscious state were my health problems. What I aim for with this book is that you will be snapped into a state of empowerment if you aren't already there and out of the status quo, without having to go through the suffering that woke me up. I want to fast track you into a state of constant growth and clarity. I ask people in my clinic what it would take for them to wake up. Some people only learn from hard lessons, but the easiest way to learn is by starting to question what you want, look forward, and act now!

Maybe you're reading this book because you've had a life-changing experience that has made you more aware of it. Or maybe you're living a day-to-day life where you're not really aware of where it's heading and you want to change that. Maybe you realise there is more to life than your job. Perhaps you aren't really making a living, you're making a "dying," or you aren't really happy because you aren't realising your potential—you're living day to day with no joy or happiness. You want more inspiration and more connection to your higher self, to truly live the life you want.

Take a moment to think about what you would regret not doing if you died in seven days. Would you be happy with what you're doing in your life right now, or is there something you would regret not doing? If money was not a factor, how would you spend your time? These questions are designed to help you think about what you really want from your life.

I decided one day, slumped over the wheel of a forklift in a cool room, that I had to do something for work that I loved every single day. The next morning I handed in my resignation. I was twenty-one years old and decided I was never again going to work in a job that I did not like. I was never going to wake up and regret going to work. Unfortunately, not many people can say that. There are a lot of people who do jobs they hate purely for money, jobs that kill their spirit and drive them into the ground. But life is not two days a week, it's seven. You have to be happy every day. The first step to being happy and achieving your potential is to begin being healthy right now!

Learning about natural medicine has given me the tools, the energy, and the edge to succeed. It has put me in control of my destiny and in the driver's seat. You too can be empowered by the realisation that you have a choice whether to feel good. You have the ability to change how you feel just by understanding your body and working with it. You don't have to rely on getting sick and ending up in your doctor's surgery to address your health.

Over the following two sections of this book you will be provided with some tools to start you on the road to reaching your potential. This is the first step in providing an overhaul of your life and removing the things that are blocking this breakthrough. You now know why your health matters—*because it gives you the clarity to connect to your telos and to live a life in alignment with your purpose and happiness.*

In the next section we will focus on how you can improve your health, and in the final section you will develop an individual plan to start you on your journey.

Diagram C

The H-C-T Connection

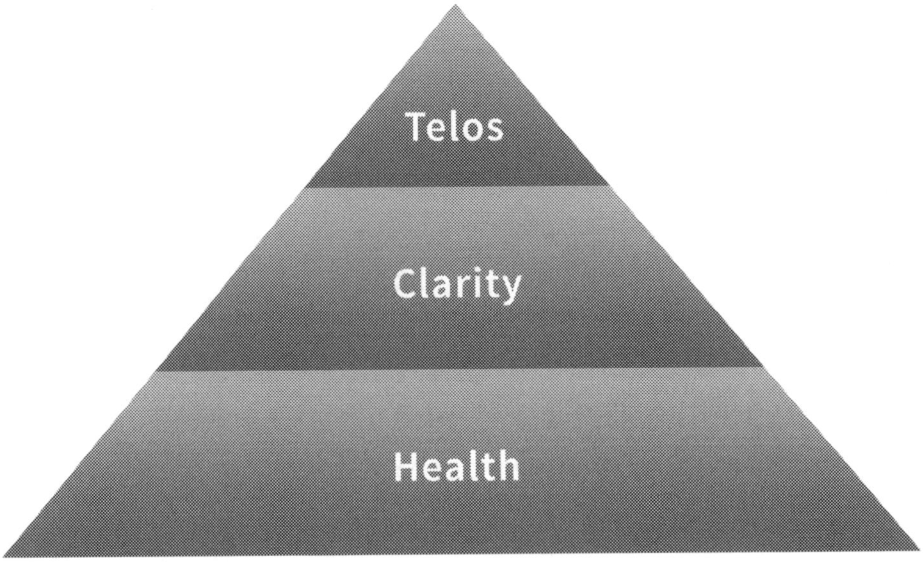

28

Part 2

Chapter 4

Understanding Yourself as an Individual

Too many self-help books and programs seek to provide a one-size-fits-all solution to living a happy life. While some general truths apply to all people, such as we are happiest when we are connected to achieving our telos, we also must realise that our health is crucial to having the clarity necessary to even understand our telos. It is clear that we must adopt an individual approach that reflects our individual health and well-being needs.

We each have our own story. The father of Western medicine, Hippocrates—the source of the Hippocratic Oath that has guided the ethics of doctors for millennia—stated, "It is more important to know what sort of person has a disease than to know what sort of disease a person has."

For me, realising the importance of understanding self was a major discovery. One day I woke up and it dawned on me that to really heal myself, I first needed to understand myself. This was an epiphany, and it will be for you as you get clarity on who you are, what you need, and what you want.

Into my head popped a revelation that I discovered and have lived by ever since that moment in 1999: *One only heals when sense of self is recognised.*

I became more aware of that as I better understood myself, and as a result, the better I could heal myself. At the time I was working and living in a practice in Bondi Junction. I had a deal where I was given a room and a place from which to practice. I had a moment where I was trying to think of what to do for a patient while also trying to figure out what was going on with my own health. There was something not quite right. I felt the only way that I could move forward was to really understand myself.

Understanding myself became a key to healing myself, and I realised that if I was going to help others heal, I had to help them understand themselves too. Even more than this it hit home for me that to be an effective practitioner, I had to understand myself because a healer must heal himself or herself in order to heal others. A healer must be healing. It's the energy from healing that you pass on to the patient.

I sat back and thought, *You really can only heal if you recognise what is going on in yourself and are able to apply what you need.* This understanding also opens you up to identifying and embracing things that come your way and trusting your instincts in knowing what is right for yourself. If you suppress your instincts, then you're not allowing yourself to come through.

As you read this section, it explains how you can be healthy, how you can find and connect with your telos, and how you can live a fulfilled life. Remember that this is ultimately about you as an individual. You are unique, and so is your path to living a happy life.

I want you to reflect on yourself. I want you to get excited about learning about yourself. I'm not going to just dictate a set of things that you should do to find happiness. As you read, you need to reflect. You need to seek to understand yourself. While I will give you information and advice to help you start living toward a happy life, in the end you need to be proactive both now as you read and in the future as you implement the plan this book will help you to develop.

Who we are is also an evolutional process. For example, our bodies do not respond to diet and exercise at forty like they did at fourteen. We don't need to be concerned by change, but what we do need is to be constantly reflecting on who we are in that moment. You don't get to answer the question once and for all. We need to reflect inwardly and honestly ask ourselves who we are, what we are feeling, and what we need. If you ask yourself the right questions, your intuition will give you the right answer. You just have to learn to trust it.

There are many factors that make us who we are: genetics, blood type, upbringing, personality, character, history, and environment. For this reason no book can tell you exactly what you should do to heal yourself and reach your full potential. You need to learn to question your own body and listen to it. A lot of the time healing comes down to listening to yourself more than anything else. Later I will give you strategies on how to assess yourself to make better choices in your life and for your health.

On a daily basis many people realise that what is good for the goose is not always good for the gander. The reason is that we are all individual and all have different needs that should be honoured.

Here are a few of the things that make us who we are:

- blood type and rhesus factor;

- our genetic origin;

- genetic predisposition to disease including gene mutations called singular nuclear polymorphism (snips);

- spiritual beliefs;

- astrological birth date;

- environment during upbringing;

- family dynamics and position in family;

- place (such as country) of birth;

- level of spiritual growth;

- social beliefs; and

- your internal representation based on your life experiences

The list goes on.

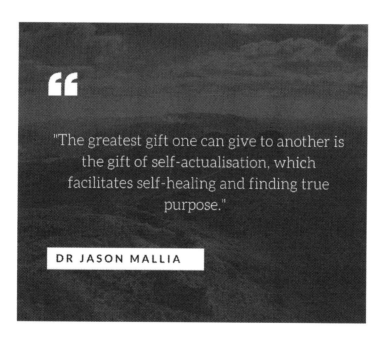

"The greatest gift one can give to another is the gift of self-actualisation, which facilitates self-healing and finding true purpose."

DR JASON MALLIA

While there are many aspects to who we are, a helpful insight into your individuality is provided by genetics. If we understand our genetic origin, it helps us understand why we function a certain way. Genetics tells us a person's history so we can see where they come from and what cards they have been dealt. How you play those cards depends on what you do with your lifestyle and environment. For example, if someone is predisposed to cardiovascular disease but runs every day, takes fish oil supplements, and does all the right things, that condition is less likely to be a problem in his or her life. But if someone gets diagnosed because he or she hasn't led the right lifestyle, then genetics can explain why that person may have gotten the disease while someone doing the same things doesn't.

The study of how lifestyle, environmental factors, and our choices influence our genes is called epigenetics. Research has shown that these factors can act as a switch, turning genes on and off based on our lifestyle choices. This external influence is responsible for up to 80 percent of our health status, while our genetic makeup only represents the other 20 percent of who we are.

Genetics still gives us an understanding of who we are and where we come from. It lets us know our weaknesses and strengths. For example, I learned about my genetic profile through extensive genetic testing and it told me that my body was suited to mixed endurance exercise, so that explains why I was suited to rugby league. With rugby league training, you run for eighty minutes while also lifting weights and doing strength work. It's not just sprints. You're running around, then sprinting, then stopping, and then driving somebody into the ground. Unlike myself, some people are more geared specifically toward endurance exercise and others toward highly intensive activity.

If you understand your genetics, you can work with your strengths, build up your weaknesses, and be leaps and bounds ahead of everyone else. It enables you to reach your potential and not be controlled by genetics. If you know your genetic profile, you can be empowered to make decisions that are more accurate and specific to your health requirements. It's not only what you are exhibiting now that you have to worry about as this is merely an expression of where you are in your current state of health. Of course, symptoms and the way a person may feel need to be addressed, but you never really understand why a person is unwell unless he or she examines the inner workings of his or her body. That is usually linked to genetics.

Fortunately, our genetics are not a life sentence. Once you have your DNA blueprint analysed, you can understand how those genes can be switched on and off based on what you do with your lifestyle. Advances in genomics have made it affordable for people to have their own genome sequenced and analysed. I have done this for myself to better understand my body. After countless years of healing myself, understanding my genetics gave me further insight. I have also had many patients in my clinic undergo this process. However, it is not absolutely necessary to go to that extent to get a general understanding of your genetics and to begin making changes to your diet and lifestyle. Just knowing your blood type can give you some insight and guidance in this area.

A person's blood type is a genetic marker and is reflective of a gene difference between the blood types. It controls certain genes and functions in our body through a linkage between our blood type and those functions. There is also a link between the way certain blood types will reject other blood types due to an incompatible transfusion—and the same holds true for food. Foods contain antigens that can interact with blood. This is how the blood type diet originated. Eating the wrong food may not be as detrimental as receiving the wrong blood type, but there is still a reaction based on incompatible foods to one's blood type.

Well known naturopathic physicians Dr. Peter D'Adamo and his father, Dr. James D'Adamo, put all the pieces together. I had the honour and privilege of studying with Peter D'Adamo and speaking on behalf of the *New York Times* best-selling author of *Eat Right for Your Type*. What blood type you have determines what diseases you may have a higher risk factor for. In fact, hospital statistics support the fact that certain diseases are more prevalent in certain blood types. For example, type A people have a higher incidence of cancer than any other blood type. When researchers studied this, they questioned why one blood type may have more of a risk factor over another for the development of a particular disease. They measured parameters such as blood clotting factors, cortisol levels, and enzyme functions, and what they found were differences consistent with the individual blood types. They found a link between the gene (9q34) that determines your blood type and links to various functions of our bodies that are controlled by our blood type gene. This therefore suggests that not only do we function differently based on our blood type gene but also that our health requirements are different based on our blood type.

Blood type is a good starting point for most people for understanding their genetic individuality. A person's blood type is a genetically determined scientific marker that individualises each person from one another. I highly recommend that people adopt a diet system based upon their blood type to utilise specific foods and nutrients that are suited to their particular blood type, in order to enhance or improve their overall health status.

Eating specifically to your own personal needs is a crucial element for achieving optimum health. However, in today's fast-paced society, achieving optimum health can be a rather difficult task. The blood type diet, on the other hand, is an easy-to-follow system for anyone wanting to eat more specifically for their individual needs. It is a system that enables the individual to build awareness of foods and how they affect us positively and negatively.

Not only is it a diet but a fully integrated system in itself, using the science of blood type and the best of complementary health care. By understanding individuality through blood type, specific treatments can be tailored to the patient.

Over the past decade I have successfully integrated blood type principles into my practice, whether it be in a modified diet for weight loss, a modified disease management program, or simply for well-being. The blood type principles are at the foundation of all of my health programs. I feel this approach has been crucial over the years.

The fact of the matter is that we as human beings have lost touch with ourselves. We rely too heavily on the media and product advertising to understand what is good for us. We are told eat this cereal, it gives you this benefit, or eat this muesli bar because it gives you that benefit.

Doctors generally tell us to follow certain diets for particular health problems. For instance, heart disease patients are told to cut out saturated fats and reduce cholesterol in their diets. These recommendations are all fine, but we need to get more specific in order to increase our healing potential.

Your body is so sophisticated that it tells you what it needs. Most people who stumble across the blood type diet resonate with it because it makes sense. It resonates with our instincts that tell us what is good for us. This helps people get back in tune with themselves. The failure to do this is usually the reason they get sick in the first place. In order for people to get back to optimum health, they must listen to what feels best for themselves as individuals, and getting blood type specific, while it's not the be all, end-all, is a great place to start!

A key reason to use the blood type diet is to guide you back to one that is more suitable to your nutritional needs. When our gut flora is in balance we do this naturally, but when our gut health is out of balance, it can be difficult to understand the messages our gut is sending to our brain. When your digestive system or gut microbiome (gut bacteria) is in balance, you will crave what your body needs, but the opposite can happen when it is out of balance. For example, a bug such as Candida in your digestive system can cause you to crave sugar because it needs sugar to survive. When you get rid of the bug, the craving disappears. The healthier your gut microbiome is, the more reliable your body will become in telling you what it needs. To get it balanced, the blood type diet is invaluable.

Blood type is a genetically determined marker that gives us one level of individuality that we can work with to enhance our health. Often, many people find they are doing the right thing most of the time and that the blood type diet merely helps them fine-tune what they consume. However, some people are not eating blood type specific foods and have lost sense of themselves to a degree, often resulting in poor gut health, poor immunity, and frequent chronic issues.

In addition to knowing your blood type, it is helpful to reflect on your character or personality traits. This comes from understanding how you function in certain situations. Knowing your character lets you know how you are going to respond. When I treat a client, if I see he or she is the stubborn type, then I'm going to be very conscious that I'm not going to push in a way that's going to get him or her to dig in his or her heels. But if a patient is the passive type, I might have to encourage him or her twice as hard. When I understand someone's character, it helps me determine what he or she is best going to respond to. The same goes for you understanding your own character.

From my experience a person's character is one of two types: one that is goal driven and easily motivated to act, or one who is contemplative and needs extra motivation to make a change.

The strength of goal-driven people is that they follow protocol and execute the plan. Their weakness is that they can become too rigid in their approach, which can actually become an issue in itself. They can be so fixated on getting results that they push themselves too hard and then realise they're driving themselves into the ground. They put their blinkers on and don't stop until they get what they want, but sometimes this means they come up against obstacles because they can try and push through things rather than allowing them to unfold. They can struggle with tuning into what their body needs day to day. They like things to be black and white, but things rarely are. They will do everything you tell them to, but they don't always have the ability to adapt and change.

Contemplative people tend to be unsure of things. They want to think about them. They want to make the right decisions. They don't want to rush into something. The problem is, they procrastinate a lot. It's good to make the right decision, but too much contemplation can be negative because you're not taking action.

Interestingly, you can almost split these characters up by blood type: it's the type As versus the Os. The Os are more driven, the hunters trying to get what they want, whereas the As are a little more sophisticated. They are more likely to contemplate ideas before they rush out and do something.

The other blood types haven't been studied as much as those two from an emotional point of view because the majority of the world's population is either O or A. About 11 percent of the population are Bs and 4 percent are ABs, compared to 45 percent of Os and 40 percent of As. Bs tend to be the type that are emotionally centred. ABs are a mixture of A and B. They are slightly emotionally centred but are not as driven as Os.

Understanding your individuality through your blood type and character can help you develop a program that can empower you to live a happy life. However, what is often the determining factor in whether this program is successful is whether the person really wants to get better. You might assume that everyone would always want to get better, but often that isn't the case. Sometimes people aren't ready to begin living happy lives just yet. Sometimes people need to go through pain, sickness, and suffering (just like I did) before they really want to get better and make the decision to do so. When people know what they want and why they want it, they're more likely to be motivated regardless of who they are as an individual.

Fortunately, our bodies are on the side of wanting us to be the best version of ourselves, and our subconscious minds are orchestrating the whole process. When we are not listening to ourselves, our bodies often create disease or crisis to try to wake us up. This is what repeatedly happened to me.

The symptoms caused by disease make you ask questions, and then you start searching for answers. It's a reaction based on something going wrong. Most people don't go to a doctor unless something's wrong. Most people don't ask questions about what is going on in their body until they don't feel right. Symptoms lead to questions about your inner goings on, but they also lead to questions about what is going on in your life. What could have caused this? Why am I sick when my friend next door who does the same things is not? I want to save you from the suffering I had to endure to finally realise the health we can truly have—a health that is so much more than just an absence of something wrong.

Chapter 5

Natural and Mainstream Medicine

When you have searched your own soul and have gained clarity, no one knows you better than yourself. This doesn't mean that there's no value in welcoming an outside perspective, such as a professional expert in the field. Understanding about your individuality and what you want will help lay the foundation to develop your own program. This book aims to help you break through and start you on the path to living the life you dream of. Getting on this path will impact your life in ways you may not have even realised were possible. At times, we all need expert guidance to help us along the way. It is important to understand that this book cannot be a substitute for the guidance that a natural healthcare practitioner can provide based on their expertise and your specific situation. This book is designed as a guide, but a practitioner can help you to fine tune your understanding of yourself and to get better results from what you chose to do.

Seeking the help of naturopathic/integrative practitioners and mainstream practitioners is important and at times crucial. Before continuing in this section, to examine the fundamentals of getting your body functioning and to explore the five elements of health and wellness, I want to briefly discuss these different approaches to medicine and their importance. I am an advocate of integrative medicine and believe that the best result for you is achieved by combining both.

Mainstream medicine is largely about understanding the body through its anatomy, physiology, and pathogenesis, and then applying strategies such as drugs and surgery to achieve a desired result, usually including the removal or masking of symptoms.

Natural medicine is not only about treating symptoms. It does not utilise surgery or drugs. It does treat symptoms, but its focus is on the underlying cause of the illness. When mainstream medicine doesn't understand the cause of a symptom, it is often said that the cause is largely unknown. There is always a cause and driver to illness. Natural medicine looks beyond what are recognised causes for known diseases and illnesses and will consider factors such as the environment (toxic, pathogenic, or microbial), stress, diet, and genetics. Natural medicine practitioners are trained to look deeply for the underlying reasons of illness and do not generalise that all people with a certain disease has the same cause.

There may be many causes that could have contributed to a person getting a disease or a set of symptoms, and it will be different in each person—based on the person's individual genetics, blood type, and a whole range of other things that make us susceptible to disease. Certain diseases have been shown to be more prominent in certain blood types, but unfortunately, mainstream medicine most often overlooks this information. It is concerned with finding the disease process and then trying to understand how to improve the symptoms. There are not many situations where mainstream practitioners treat the underlying causes.

Natural medicine seeks to understand the fundamental reasons why the body is malfunctioning and then applies treatments based on that particular area—whether it be diet, supplements, exercise, or detoxification. Natural medicine seeks to address imbalances in the body. This focus on the treatment of the whole person is about treating their vitality and is the key difference between it and mainstream medicine.

Prescribing pharmaceuticals will often help address symptoms in the short term, but without treating a patient's vitality over time, it will decrease and create further stresses on the body. Drugs can be great for a short period of time, but often dosages need to be increased or the medication changed and this starts to affect the body. However, the more you treat a person's vitality—strengthening their energy, digestion, and immunity—the more their body is able to heal itself.

The best approach is integrative between natural and mainstream medicine. An integrative approach gives you an assessment of the condition, and you then look at what short-term interventions are needed to improve the person's condition. For example, if the person is in pain, the first port of call is pain relief. If the condition is life threatening, then the first intervention is using mainstream medicine to get him or her out of trouble.

Mainstream medicine excels at treating acute conditions, where symptoms appear and change rapidly, such as with a broken bone, serious infection, or an asthma attack. Once the patient is out of trouble, it doesn't make sense to keep him or her on acute treatment if there is an underlying chronic condition, which has developed and worsened over an extended period of time. This is where natural medicine excels, in the chronic management of illnesses, such as the osteoporosis or the asthma that was the cause of the acute condition.

A danger with a mainstream, symptom-focused approach to chronic conditions is that patients can enter into a pain-treatment cycle, and eventually this creates more problems. By treating symptoms rather than the underlying condition, a patient's healing can actually be held back.

Diagram D

The Pain-Treatment Cycle

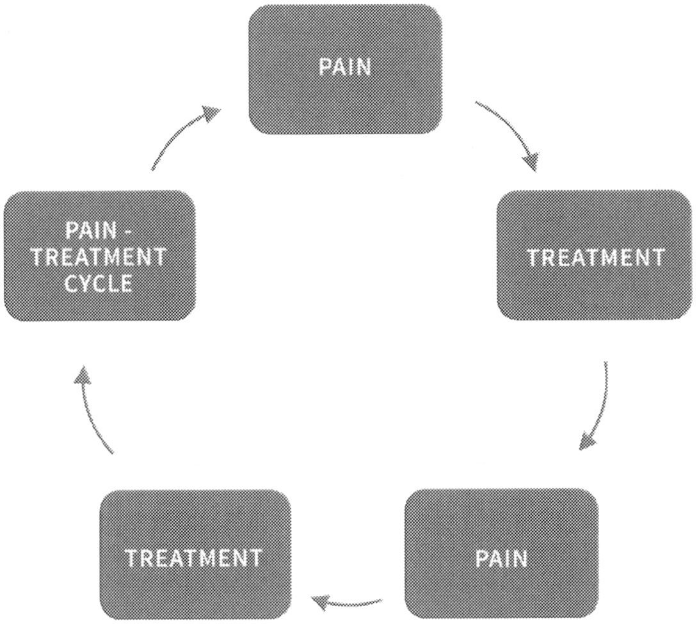

PAIN

TREATMENT

PAIN - TREATMENT CYCLE

TREATMENT

PAIN

Do you want to be someone who just gets some symptom relief and then comes back again for more? Or do you want to fix your problem? Do you want to get to the bottom of your problem? It is better in the long term to understand why you have back pain than to just take medicine to relieve it. When the medicine wears off, the pain will just come back again. We want to break this cycle and then help you to move forward. There's always an underlying reason for a condition. Natural medicine provides a different mind-set to a symptoms-focused approach.

Addressing the underlying reasons for a condition may seem to be the obvious choice for treatment, but patients can be reluctant to take this approach because it involves hard work. You may have to change what you eat and drink, how you exercise, and your environment. This is harder than simply taking medicine, but medicine alone cannot offer long-term relief and provide the foundation of health that is necessary to live a completely happy life.

Despite this, I want to reiterate the importance of mainstream medicine to be used in conjunction with natural medicine. For example, mainstream medicine can do great wonders to save someone's life by replacing a kidney or heart. However, while in certain circumstances it is definitely needed, in other cases surgery should be the last option, not the first and only option looked at.

In countries such as Australia where natural medicine practitioners are not MDs, unlike in the United States, I believe everyone should consult their mainstream doctor first when in need of treatment. The doctor should then refer the patient to a natural medicine practitioner if additional treatment is needed. If they can't find the underlying problem with the patient, they should provide symptom relief where appropriate and then refer them to a naturopath, an acupuncturist, a chiropractor, or other natural medicine practitioners as appropriate. Unfortunately, this doesn't happen regularly enough, and patients are just left with symptom treatment while their underlying problem is not addressed.

Chapter 6

The Five Hidden Drivers of Disease

Natural medicine seeks to understand the cause of illness. Research has shown that most chronic diseases have a driver connected to the disease. These drivers include toxicity, stress, pathogens, inflammation, and poor nutrition.

Diagram E

Five Drivers of Disease

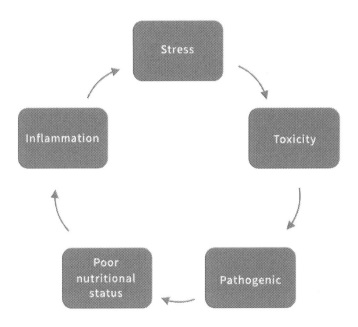

These have all been linked to the progression of certain conditions. For example, in the chronic autoimmune disease multiple sclerosis, certain microbes have been shown to be present in sufferers, leading to a dysregulation of their immune systems. It is important to understand the existence of these drivers so that you can implement a plan to counteract them and improve your condition. The purpose of this book is not to focus on these drivers but rather to bring them to your attention so that you can know whether you may need to further investigate one or more of them.

Chapter 7
The Key Fundamentals of Healing

It is a well-established fact that for health, wellness, and happiness, the three main areas that need to be in balance are the mind, body, and spirit. Within these three main areas are six components of your body that you must be mindful of to be in a state of health and wellness. These consist of biochemical, structural, physiological, emotional, mental, and life force This is indicated in diagram F.

Diagram F

The MBS Model and Their Connection

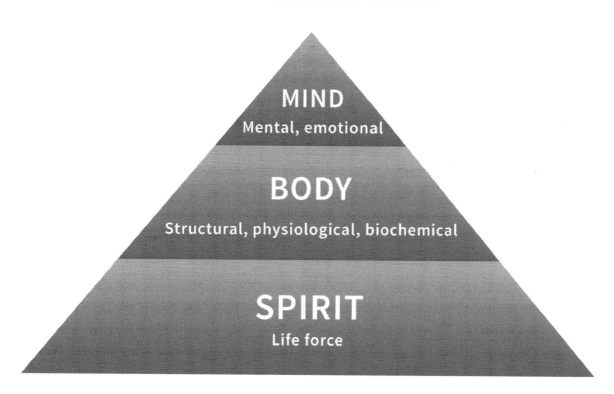

Nutritional

Without giving your body the right nutrition, it's unable to function at an optimal level. Just like a car, if you put the wrong fuel in, it will not perform on all cylinders.

Nutrition is a key foundation to your health. Your body will still function with poor nutrition, but not at the level it could. It comes down to understanding your nutritional needs and eating the right way so you get the most out of what you eat and out of your body. It's not just simply putting food in your mouth for taste; it's eating to sustain your body and using it as a way to nourish your cells. Food is meant to make you feel good, not tired. It's not meant to make you feel like you want to sleep after you eat. It's not meant to make you feel foggy. It's meant to make you feel alive. It's meant to help you produce energy in the form of ATP (adenosine triphosphate), the energy currency of the body.

Vitamins, minerals, and amino acids are responsible for thousands of biochemical reactions in the body that, when in balance, can have profound far-reaching effects on a person's well being and state of health. Many research studies will support this statement. For example, it's well established that there is a link between spina bifida and a folic acid deficiency in expecting mothers. Another example is the link between osteoporosis and vitamin D deficiency. In the northern hemisphere there is a higher incidence of autoimmune conditions such as multiple sclerosis due to a lack of sunshine and vitamin D.

Countless diseases occur as a result of poor nutrition. Another well-documented example is when sailors used to develop scurvy because they didn't have enough vitamin C on board. Just as in those times, modern medicine fails to focus on vitamins and minerals as being factors in disease. Instead, it focuses on drugs and the industrialisation of medicine rather than working with what we already know from nutrition. The last time I checked, no one died of a deficiency of Prozac!

The human body is a lot more complex than a car, and an array of nutrients are required for it to function at its best. And it's our job to try and meet those nutritional requirements. This is where food as medicine comes into play. Using nutritious food not just as something to eat but also as medicine. It can help you to feel good, support your body while under stress, and help you heal.

Structural

Recent research has shown that sitting is the most inflammatory thing a person can do. Your structure and posture are important for your overall state of health. When we think of good structure, we think of balance and alignment of our overall body structure. Often as we age, gravity works against us and we develop poor habits that affect our structure, such as incorrect sitting, standing for long periods, and undertaking activities or exercising using the wrong posture. Having sound structure is super important as a good structure keeps everything, especially organs, held in their right place. If you have a poor posture, you will potentially stress muscles, joints, nerves, and organs, which will affect the way they function. You may develop pain, discomfort, and potentially a disease. You may affect your organ health and mental state. If we create inflammation through our posture, this also drives our nervous system and creates stress. When we have aching muscles sending shockwaves through our nervous system, we create cortisol responses that then cause all sorts of negative physiological responses, even speeding up disease processes that you might have a genetic predisposition toward. This is why structure is crucial as a foundation to optimum health and function.

If you look at traditional cultures such as Indian and Chinese, they have always had a structural component to all of their health regimes. They are often seen doing yoga in India and tai chi in China. They understand the importance of structure and its connection to health. Maori healers also have a structural component to their healing methods passed down through many generations to the chosen healer in the family. I had the privilege of teaching Maori healers the Dorn method, which is a type of body alignment therapy developed in Germany. Hippocrates, the father of medicine, used manual therapy as part of his healing methods. In Roman times, the aristocracy would have massages in baths. They knew the importance of muscles not being tight but being able to function and move properly to unblock energy flow in the body. Blockages in energy flow lead to disease.

Physiological

Where the structure is like the building of the body, physiological health is what goes on inside and relate to the inner chemistry of the body. It's the inner workings of your body, such as hormonal processes, biochemical functions, enzyme productions, and organic functions.

Human beings based on physiology are generally similar across the board, despite differences according to race, culture, and individual genetic variation, but further variations can occur according to epigenetic studies. Our bodies are always trying to find balance and heal; this is called homeostasis. This relates to the balance of hormones, balance of digestive juices, balance of ph and acid levels in your body—your body is always trying to find that balance—but there are negative factors that will trigger overproduction or underproduction, effecting this balance. There can be excess states or deficiency states. The body needs to be in balance on a biochemical level for everything to be functioning properly. For example, someone that overproduces stomach acid as a result of having too much coffee might start to get acid reflux or gastritis. That is going to upset the acid balance and maybe cause a problem further down the track.

Emotional/Mental/Life Force

According to scientific research, ancient healing philosophy, and my own clinical research, our mental, emotional, and spiritual health is paramount to health and overall well-being. Recent scientific studies can now explain how it is all linked, and using this understanding can help us to be balanced on all levels. In fact, a new study of these interconnections links our brains, guts (digestive systems), and immune systems, known as the gut/brain/immune axis. Diagram G (below) shows how when one is out of balance, the other is also out of balance and the downstream causes that can affect our clarity and happiness.

According to the work of psychiatric professor Michael Myers, many depressive disorders also have underlying roots in the gut. In fact, up to 80 percent of the feel-good neurotransmitter, serotonin, is produced in the gut! Therefore, if we have decreased amounts of serotonin, the gut may be partly responsible. Our emotional health depends on it. Furthermore, our gut immune system and gut microbiome (flora) plays a central role in the balance of our serotonin and brain health. Early naturopaths and Eastern medicine practitioners have long known the link and now the research is there to support this. As mentioned earlier, finding clarity and happiness relies heavily on our state of health (diagram C, the HCT connection, illustrates this).

Spiritual connection and connecting to our purpose is also dependent on clarity and health via the gut/brain/immune connection. Therefore, to simplify, they are all dependent on each other and can influence our clarity and purpose.

Diagram G

Gut/Brain/Immune Axis

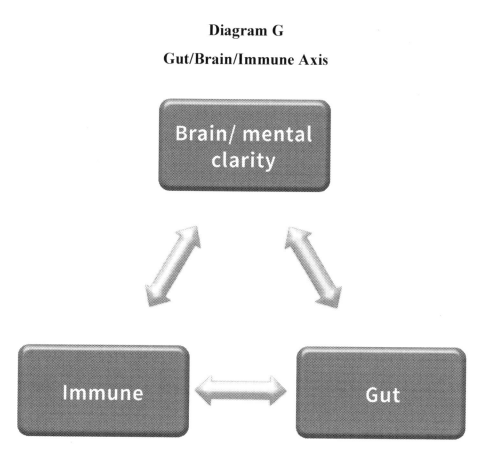

When we are out of balance or feeling stressed, it's important to start with changing the state we're in. In the next part of the book I will provide you with "mode of being" exercises that will help you do this. Additionally, if you are volatile emotionally, then you should also look into other aspects of your health such as hormonal balance, gut health, or mental health issues. It is also helpful to know what specific factors trigger certain emotions for you. The danger posed by emotions is that when they get too strong, they can override your normal senses and become disruptive to your clarity. When you lose clarity, you get disconnected from your telos and consequently achieving true happiness.

Chapter 8

The Five Elements of Health and Wellness

Over the past twenty years of clinical practice and through research and personal development, I have discovered what it takes to achieve optimum health and wellness. I have come to the conclusion that there are five essential elements. In my practice, I have developed the five elements of wellness which are known as the five As to wellness.

These five elements are essential for you to implement in your life and underpin your plan for a happy and healthy life. You will create a plan for yourself in the next part of the book.

Element 1—Attitude

To achieve your goal, you must have the right mind-set and attitude. In my clinic I often start off a session by asking a client some questions, such as, "Why are you here? What is it you want to achieve? Why do you want to achieve?" This is a crucial part of the process as this helps us gain clarity on what has motivated him or her to come to my clinic. Once we have established this, people are more likely to get on board with the absolute intention and commitment to follow through on their program. You must be ready and in the right headspace. You can't do anything without having your mind focused and engaged. When you're focused, you become unstoppable. Focus puts your energy into the direction you are heading and you are rewarded. Energy in equals energy back to you.

However, you must begin with the desire to succeed. For the plan you will create for yourself in the next part of the book, you must be committed to living your dream. If you don't have the right attitude, you will just receive this advice and it will go out the window because you're not going to apply it.

To improve your attitude and commitment to your plan, it's important to first be clear about what you want and what's going to motivate you to get your mind on the job. For example, say your key objective is to have more energy. Ask yourself what you will get out of having more energy. Perhaps it's to fulfil a dream to run a marathon. With this answer, tap into the positives that can come out of implementing a plan to give you more energy, and this will motivate you to have the right mind-set to complete your daily rituals to achieve it.

When you understand the connection between following your daily rituals and achieving what you want, it can help motivate you to take small steps toward your larger goals. There's no point developing a plan if you're not going to change what you do day-to-day. For instance, if you're still going to drink alcohol and eat junk food every day of the week, this will be detrimental to your end result. Also, you can't maintain that behaviour and still expect to feel energetic and function at an optimal level in order to achieve your life goals.

Getting your attitude and mind-set right comes from focusing on your "why," such as wanting to feel energetic so you can play with your children and be the parent you desire to be. You don't need to worry about how you will achieve your goals at first because if you understand how the why and the how are going to happen. You need to start with the correct attitude and mind-set. Working on this every day will become a crucial part of your success.

In improving your attitude and mind-set, it helps to focus on what you want rather than what you don't want and create what you desire.

In the plan you will create, you will understand the importance of creating daily rituals and affirmations. These will give you a positive attitude toward what you're doing. You will also add gratitude to your daily rituals, giving thanks everyday for what you have. This gratitude will propel you further toward getting what you do want. These rituals will plant the seeds and grow into healthy behaviours.

Diagram H

Progression to Your Telos

MOTIVATION

Element 2—Assessment

The next step is assessing your current level of health. I have included the integrated health questionnaire in the appendix to help you focus on areas where you're lacking or where your blocks are and to know where your strengths lie. We can use our strengths and think about how we can overcome our weaknesses. This becomes an individualised understanding of your own health. Some simple questions to consider in addition to the questionnaire are:

- When was the last time you really felt well?
- What have you done to try to improve your wellness?
- Do you have enough time in the day to do what you want to do?
- Do you have the energy or motivation to complete what you set out to do?
- Are you sleeping well?
- Is there a lot on your mind?
- What lies between now and ultimately being happy?
- What blocks you on any level from achieving your health and life goals?

Diagram I

Road Block to Success

Further Testing

Additionally, there are a number of other tests you can access through an integrative healthcare professional. These include full blood counts and microscopic analysis, genetic tests, and integrative pathology assessments. Each case may vary in the level of assessment required because some people may require more thorough integrative medical testing. With this book you are only taking the first step in assessing yourself, but a much more comprehensive assessment is available through consulting a practitioner and should be considered. The more information you have about yourself the better, as you will be able to target more specifically the imbalances that you need to work on, particularly if you have a pressing health concern.

Element 3—Advice

In a clinical situation, my approach is to create an action plan for you based on information collated from all of your assessments, such as full blood testing, full body screenings, supplementary medical tests, and genetic testing. Then we develop what is known as a report of findings (ROF). From this ROF, an action plan and strategy are developed.

The goal of this book is to guide you in the creation of your very own action plan. Of course there are limitations, such as the assessment part, as an action plan created by a practitioner would be more specifically tailored. However, this book will start you in the right direction to achieve a higher state of health and wellness.

An action plan is important because it is your strategy for achieving your goals. Trying to achieve health and happiness without a plan would be like going to war and just throwing all your soldiers at the enemy rather than having a strategy. You must understand what you're dealing with and then apply a program to it. The plan you will create for yourself in the next part of the book will address various aspects of your life including attitude, diet, lifestyle, exercise, and stress management.

Element 4—Application

This is the implementation and doing the rituals of the plan you will create for yourself. An important tool in implementation is to set milestones toward each of the goals that you want to achieve and to tick them off as you pass each one, making you feel more empowered to go to the next level. In fact, patting yourself on your back keeps you motivated and hungry for more. You set short-term goals to get to your long-term goals. Once we achieve our initial goals, for example to lose ten kilograms, we then advance to another level.

If we don't implement or ritualise our plan on a daily basis to achieve our goals, we won't achieve our outcomes. We must stay committed and ensure that we stay connected to what we want. In order to keep applying ourselves, we need to keep visualising what we want and stay connected to our overall goal in the process. Mind-set techniques that you will learn about in the breakthrough program will keep you on track and focused.

Sometimes people stop applying themselves because there's something in their state of mind that has changed, something that says, "I'm not going to do this today." In the next part of this book I will share techniques for changing your mode of being (MOB) when you find it is not in the right place. Your mental state can be changed within seconds just by simple controlled breathing, movement, or physical activity, getting some sunshine, eating healthy food, or drinking water. When you haven't applied yourself on a particular day, it's important to look back and see why. Succeeding is 90 percent mental. It's all about mastering your mind-set, which is connected to your telos—what you truly want at the end of the day. You must make it your mission to stay connected to achieving your telos.

Element 5—Advancement

Advancement is the stage where you have changed into a better version of yourself based on the five As of wellness. Your objective now is to transcend the old version of yourself and set new goals based. As you implement your plan and achieve your goals, you will find that you become more connected to who you are and what you really want. You will also have a better understanding of your body. Your new plan will reflect this greater level of knowledge and better-refined goals.

Diagram J

Five Elements of Health and Wellness

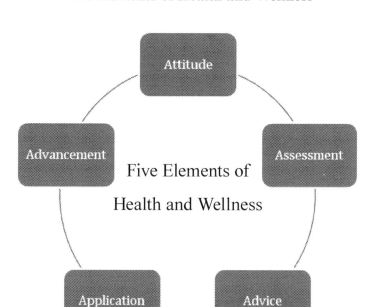

In the advancement stage, you are in a position to keep yourself on track for living a happy and healthy life and achieving your telos. You have been through the process of doing what you need to do to get healthy. You know now what it takes to become your own healer, and you know when you need to take action to change your lifestyle. At this stage you are able to identify problems as they arise.

The main challenge for you, and for others who complete my programs, is to not slip into old patterns as a result of not holding yourself accountable. It's like a tug of war between the best and worst versions of yourself. The better version knows what is best for you and tries to make decisions based on this, but the worst version tries to sabotage and get in the way of your authentic natural path. The key here is to let the better version win and identify when the worst version is trying to take hold. Allow yourself to not be perfect and get back on track if you slip. Progression over perfection!

When you have applied yourself and reached your goals and become closer to your telos, you need to take time to congratulate yourself for the achievement. From this new space it is time to refocus and think about what you want. At this point it is important to create new goals as there will always to be a gap between where you're at and where you want to be. We never stop the creative process. We continually move our goals further ahead.

For advancement, it is about using all those former steps to set up the next stage. Now that you have advanced once and you have got the confidence to advance again, you can start thinking about your next stage. You know how you feel from having achieved your goal. Now what do you want? Start the process again.

Advancing is not just moving forward in your health but in your life. I want you to live an amazing life. When you're not healthy you have to limit your choices, but when you are healthy you can live a life with more freedom—though you always need to be mindful of the foundation of your health.

Chapter 9

Setting You up for Success

I want to set you up for success, but first, here are some key reasons people fail to achieve their goals. I want to give you some tips to help you break through and succeed.

The main reasons people may fail in achieving their goals are

- ➤ not being organised with their rituals and strategies;
- ➤ not aligning daily rituals with goals;
- ➤ not identifying blocks to healing and progress;
- ➤ not understanding what they are doing and why;
- ➤ not understanding themselves and their telos;
- ➤ not seeing the importance of health as a foundation to clarity and purpose;
- ➤ not strong enough authentic motivation and not understanding their 'why';
- ➤ not ignoring negative factors that enter their minds;
- ➤ not having a positive mind-set and spending time procrastinating;
- ➤ not making themselves a priority;
- ➤ not focusing on high-level priorities and focusing on low level priorities;
- ➤ not ready to be a better version of themselves;
- ➤ not focusing on the solution;
- ➤ not realising how much happier and healthier they can be;
- ➤ making excuses and telling themselves stories about why they can't;
- ➤ lacking focus and drive;
- ➤ lacking motivation and direction;
- ➤ trying to be perfect and putting far too much pressure on themselves; and
- ➤ quitting when the going gets tough.

Do any of these sound like you? If you resonate with any of the above, you're not alone. Many of us have struggled with these reasons, including me! The most important thing is to understand yourself through this process and be mindful of this before you start your program. This will nip a potential issue in the bud early through awareness and understanding. If you understand the issue, we can address it. One of the key reasons people fail is because they really don't know what they want and why. While it won't always be crystal clear early in the program, as you progress, stay focused and have faith that it will become clearer. The key is to stay open to the fact that for you to succeed you need to be connected at some level to what you want and why as this will be a key motivator.

Unfortunately, as a result of human conditioning, many of us only take action when we face a crisis such as illness. Usually it is then that we find the motivation to take control. Rather than needing something negative to motivate us, we can find positive motivation in being connected to our why, our telos, and our ultimate goals.

The essence is focusing on the solution and what we want and to not allow the fear of where we might end up if we don't succeed to be the motivator. I want you to prioritise living a happy and healthy life right now without illness being your driver.

When our minds have us committed to living a happy and healthy life and we are connected to our what and why, our superficial reasons for abandoning our plans (e.g., lack of money, tiredness, geographic restrictions, or other commitments) become easier to overcome. We all know from our own experience that if we want something badly enough, almost nothing can get in the way of achieving it. Stay connected to your telos and you will execute your plan.

When you're connected to what you want, everything associated with your telos comes into your consciousness and helps you progress. Understanding how your brain is wired will help you understand how it all works. In our brain we have what is known as the reticular activating system, or RAS. Its primary function is to receive sensory information such as what we see, hear, or touch and then filter out information that is not required and to alert us of information that is important and bring it into our consciousness. Let's say one day you decide that you want to buy a new black sports car and have put this on your radar. Your brain has now registered this as something to pay attention to. The very next day you start noticing billboards, magazines, and Facebook pictures of the car you desire. Has this ever happened to you? Your RAS system has made your reticular matter in your brain conscious of your needs and desires and is connecting you to everything associated with them.

It's quite interesting when you can utilise this part of your brain to your advantage. When I first met my partner, she asked me how it was that when I need to get up early to play golf that I would always wake up on time without an alarm clock. My method is to tell myself what time I need to wake up and the RAS takes over.

The same applies if you want to succeed in this program. If we stay connected to our short-term and long-term goals, our RAS system starts paying attention to things connected to it, making it easier for us to succeed. For example, you've decided that your goal is to run a marathon, and for this you need a number of items, including new sneakers. You become conscious that you would like to purchase a pair that gives you maximum performance and comfort. Your RAS system now recognises this and starts to filter and bring to your consciousness everything associated with your needs. You then see an advertisement with a famous runner promoting the latest technology and performance in shoes. Being aware of the RAS system and how it works enables you to use it to your advantage and help you with your plan.

Diagram K

The RAS System

"THE RAS SYSTEM FILTERS SENSORY INFORMATION AND ASSOCIATES IT WITH OUR NEEDS, GOALS, DREAMS, AND DESIRES WITHIN OUR CONSCIOUSNESS."

This doesn't mean that some days won't be harder than others, but that's why you will develop daily rituals as part of your plan. Creating awesome rituals is helpful for achieving the success you desire. It's important to ritualise your goals. It's important to ritualise being grateful. It's important to make exercise and eating well part of your everyday lifestyle.

As you get healthier and gain more clarity in your life, you may also be confronted with emotions and feelings that you had previously suppressed. When these surface, it can be tempting to quit because it is often hard to address and process these things. You will have to be honest with yourself about what these emotions represent.

The biggest change I ever made in my life was being true to myself. When you are trying to find a sense of self you have to live in truth and ask yourself questions and you will have to answer these questions honestly. Honouring your true self can change the fabric of your whole life. As a result, you may no longer associate with certain people, you may no longer do certain things, and your environment may change. Some people may never find their telos because they are not being true to themselves. Living our truth causes us to change and grow, and this may include doing things differently than before.

When people become clearer and healthier, they reach new heights. But in order to reach your potential, you can't tell yourself lies or you'll never find your path. Things will arise that you don't want to deal with. There will be deep pain for some people. If you work through it and get to the deep core of your challenges, it will help you access who you truly are. You get to know yourself through that pain and discovery.

The truth comes out when you ask yourself the right questions and you answer them truthfully. In my travels, I constantly asked myself questions such as what do I want? What is my purpose? What do I want to be like? Who do I want to be?

I went through a lot of upheaval, answered truthfully, and then I knew exactly what to do when I came back to Australia and committed to transforming my life.

Fortunately, once you begin to get a taste of the happiness and health that is waiting for you, it will become increasingly easy to stick to the plan. You won't want to go back to your old life and the old version of you. You will want to move even further ahead, becoming more awesome every day!

When you're tempted to abandon your plan, take a moment to ask yourself what it is specifically that is going to stop you from achieving your goals. Ask yourself what is blocking you and what your fear is. It's important to be aware of the specific reasons you may be about to fail so that you can adequately address them. Some clients come to me and think that once I have developed a plan with them, the job is done. This is just the beginning. Once you have the plan, you need to implement and honour it. If you're struggling with this, figure out exactly what's blocking you—identify and remove it!

Sometimes the block may not be obvious. For example, I see this particularly with parents who put their children first, and this stops them from prioritising their own health and happiness. It may seem like the parents are doing the right thing by not being selfish, but if they are not healthy and happy this can have a far worse affect on their children. If parents are miserable because they aren't looking after themselves, then they may not be good to live with. They may indirectly become the problem, not the remedy. The remedy is actually for them to prioritise their own health so they become much more functional in their environment and by doing this become better parents.

When you feel your commitment slipping, keep asking yourself whether you really want to achieve those goals that you have set for yourself. If those goals aren't consistent with what you truly want in your life, then you won't have the required commitment. You need to go back and reassess your goals, your what, and your why. Similarly, if you don't think you can achieve the goals that you have set, you need to set more realistic goals for this current stage of your life. You must have at least an 80 percent belief that your goals are achievable.

Getting your mind-set right is key. Find your telos and connect with it. When I look back at all the people I have worked with, if there was one single factor that has determined whether they would succeed or not, it was whether they truly wanted what they said they wanted. It's that simple. If they truly want what they want, then nothing gets in their way.

If you're determined to get fit, you will. If you're determined to travel, you will. If you're determined to do anything, you will find a way to make it happen. You will have the strength to make the sacrifices necessary to achieve success.

Part 3

Chapter 10

Your Self-Help Plan to Transformation

I hope you've been inspired by my story and that it has shown you why it's important to make your health and wellness paramount. "Man sacrifices his health in order to make money. Then he sacrifices his money to recuperate his health. And then he is so anxious about the future that he does not enjoy the present; the result being that he does not live in the present or in the future; he lives as if he is never going to die and then dies having never really lived." James J Lachard

Therefore, the essence is to make your health a priority, so that you can have clarity and be connected to your telos and purpose and live a life in the now, full of purpose and fulfilment. You can learn from my experience and education and get fast tracked to success.

It has been my aim to teach you how you can live a healthy and happy life by understanding who you are as an individual—understanding both what your personal goals and motivations are and through the insight provided by your blood type.

I have given you an overview of natural medicine so that you can heal yourself by taking control and responsibility of putting yourself on a path to a healthy life. You have a basic understanding of the aspects of your body—nutritional, structural, physiological, and emotional/mental—and can use this understanding as a launching pad for your further development, through personal study, attending courses or seminars, or in discussion with a practitioner.

I have shared with you my five As of health and wellness: attitude, assessment, advice, application, and advancement. Finally, I have given you some tips to set you up for success.

Now it's time for action. It's time to create your own plan. I'm going to guide you through creating a personalised plan to break through the barriers and transform your life. You know why health and happiness are important. You know now what it takes to achieve them. So let's take charge and control of your life now!

Chapter 11

The Seven-Step Breakthrough to Mastering your Life

The seven-step breakthrough program is broken down into easy-to-follow steps where you will focus on mastering each component. This is how I mastered them and how I made them second nature in my own life. This is the best way to make them part of your life too. Each step runs for seven days, except for the detox phase, which runs for fourteen days. Each step builds upon your progress and moves you forward toward integrating each step as you go.

The seven steps are

1. preparation (seven days);
2. detoxification (fourteen days);
3. diet and nutrition (seven days);
4. stress management and exercise (seven days);
5. mind-set (seven days);
6. relationships (seven days); and
7. spiritual and self development (seven days).

Maybe you are already on top of some of these areas and can fast track your progress. For example, if you already follow a blood type diet, you won't need to spend too much time focusing on incorporating that into your life. Similarly, if you already exercise regularly, it may not be necessary to change what you're currently doing. Instead, you may need to refine it to be more specific to your blood type and your goal, and then you may move ahead, focusing on the next step after the allocated time. As you complete this task, you will be surprised at how easy it is to come up with a plan that will change your life. The challenge is implementing the plan and that all comes down to the quality of your daily rituals. That is why we will just focus on one step at a time as we implement this plan.

In subsequent steps you will focus on making each additional area second nature to how you live your life. Ultimately, it is developing essential daily rituals that determines the quality of our lives. They will be the difference between you achieving your goals and not achieving them. They are the habits that we can create and control that will move us toward success. They are empowering and condition us to perform physically, mentally and spiritually. What you do daily must reflect your highest values. Let's say a man has the highest values of being fit and healthy, to be an inspirational father, to be a success in business, and to be a provider for his family. However, he spends his time making poor food choices, drinking with his mates at the pub, and missing gym sessions and play dates with his kids. As a result, he becomes broke, unhealthy, unhappy, and disconnected as he is not living in accordance with his highest values. On the other hand, if he shifts his attention to working on his true values, he exercises, meets friends at the golf range to socialise, eats clean food, and spends quality time with his kids, he becomes instantly empowered. He becomes happier even though he hasn't reached his goal yet. He is feeling empowered just by taking small steps toward his goal and doing rituals in alignment with his highest values.

Some of the most influential people in the world, such as Tony Robbins, Oprah Winfrey, and Bill Gates, all have one thing in common: they all start their day with empowering rituals to enable them to be the amazing people they are and to live their purpose. They perform rituals every morning that empower them to take charge of their day. Affirmations, physical activity, meditations, gratitude, and eating well prime them before they start their day.

So now you understand the importance of daily rituals. Let's take a look at where your energy is focused. I want you to sit down with a piece of paper and divide it into two halves from top to bottom. I then want you to label the left side "highest values" and the other "lowest values." For your highest values I want you to list what is important to you and those highest values that are in alignment with your life goals or purpose. For example, you might write "wealth creation, health and vitality, property investment, and travelling." On the lowest values column, you might list things such doing the dishes, mowing the lawn, cleaning the house, balancing accounts, taking the car for service, and paying the bills.

Now observe where you spend most of your time and energy. Is your energy in the higher quadrant or lower? This will help give you clarity as to where you focus your energy.

Diagram L

Highest Vs Lowest Values

So now that you have an awareness of where your energy is currently focused, it is time to focus on our highest values and this will make us feel like we are progressing and energised rather than stagnant.

Step 1—The Preparation Phase (Seven Days)

Medical Checks and Physical Exams

Before implementing the program steps, we recommend visiting your medical doctor or naturopathic physician for a general check-up or full medical exam. My suggestion is to have your physician check on any existing health concerns such as blood sugar, cholesterol, and liver function. Also request to have a full blood count. Please notify your physician of your impending program plans. Once you have your results you can then determine if you are ready to commence. Consult your practitioner should you have any uncertainty or concerns about your current health status.

Blood Typing

Next you will need to know your blood type for the diet and exercise component. If you don't know yours, self blood typing kits are available for home use. Please see the resources page at the back of the book for details.

Self-Assessments

Assessment 1—The Integrated Health Evaluation Questionnaire

In the appendix we have provided you with an integrated health evalution questionnaire. The purpose of this assessment is to provide you with a detailed summary of your current health status. This is done at the beginning of your program to analyse the systems of your body and to understand their current state of function. Allocate the time to do this in the first week as part of your preparation. Follow the instructions as suggested in the appendix. Ensure you do this before you start the program.

Assessment 2—The Six Pillars of Health and Well-Being Self-Check

In addition, I want you to complete the self assessment of the six pillars of health and well-being. This will help you to determine the baseline of your health and well being at the start of your program and will track your progress on a weekly basis. This assessment will ensure you will progress and identify any areas that require your attention. Here is the process that I use with my patients.

First, copy diagram M (see below). For each pillar score yourself out of ten on how well you believe you are doing in each of the areas that you will be addressing in the seven-step program. As mentioned, this will build awareness of which areas you need to focus on and help you identify your strengths and weaknesses. This will also help you identify when you have progressed and allow you to pat yourself on the back to provide you with motivation!

For example, for diet and nutrition, if you believe you're doing reasonably well in this area but have room for improvement, you could score yourself with a six. We can then see that this is an area that needs improvement. However, if you scored yourself ten out of ten for exercise, then obviously less attention is required in this area. I want you to master each area, but most importantly we want progress over perfection!

Let's now create a diagram around this, similar to one I have created below. What we are aiming to do here is to get a visual of your current status. You can then use this chart to regularly check where you are at any given time. My suggestion is to do this weekly to keep yourself accountable.

Diagram M

Six Pillars of Health and Wellbeing

Preparation Phase Checklist

1. **medical exams and blood tests;**
2. **blood typing;**
3. **integrated health evaluation; and**
4. **six pillars of health and well-being self-check.**

Step 2—The Detoxification Plan (Fourteen Days)

Once you finish the preparation phase, you're ready to begin the detox.

As I stated at the beginning of this book, I believe that in order to be happy we need to live a life of purpose, a life where we're doing what we're meant to do. As we get healthier we gain more clarity and have a better understanding of our telos. Right now you may have no idea what your telos is, which is why we're going to kick-start the process with a two-week detox plan that I have developed. This is the fastest way for you to gain more clarity and connection with your telos. Even if you think you know your telos, this process will enhance your connection to it and fast track your success. Your clarity may even connect you to a higher telos that you didn't realise. Don't worry if you don't know your telos just yet. You will soon.

Detoxification is purging the body of accumulated, unwanted toxins, reducing toxins going into your system, cleansing the liver and lymphatic system, flushing out the gallbladder and kidneys, and giving the bowel movement and increasing peristalsis. It also reduces the load on our immune system, allowing it to function better. Sweating also helps encourage detoxification through the skin. In our clinic we address all those things from top to bottom, providing different detoxification solutions to focus on different areas. Remember that clarity comes from a balance of the gut/brain/immune axis.

The majority of people will benefit from doing a detoxification. In fact, I recommend it any time you feel stuck or stagnant in your life. Toxins prevent your body from operating optimally, hindering your clarity and clouding your ability to know your telos.

Detoxing Your Life

As you will see from the Integrated Health Evaluation Questionnaire (in the appendix), toxic burden doesn't just come from what we eat. We also need to be aware of our external environment to reduce our exposure to toxins. Particularly during your detox you should avoid unnecessary exposure to chemicals and pollutants. We rarely take time to consider how widespread these are and what harmful effects they may be having. Personally, I believe that toxins represent the plague of the twenty-first century.

Excessive alcohol and coffee intake, and cigarettes are the obvious toxins that people willingly put into their bodies, but the problem is exacerbated by the unnecessary use of medications, chemically based cleaning products, insect repellents, glues, plastics, paints, and toiletries. The list goes on. Add air pollution from factories and traffic and it's easy to see why our bodies struggle to keep up with the detoxification demands we place on them.

Any reduction in exposure to these things will help your body recover, especially during the detoxification recommended above.

When detoxing our bodies and our lives, it is essential to consider our emotional states, relationships, and personal belongings as these components can be sources of toxicity. Negative attitudes can make us feel toxic and unwell. If our mind-set is sound, we are more likely to be kind to our bodies, but the opposite is true when our mind is not in a balanced state.

Of equal importance is our relationships. Detoxification of self can make us aware of the current health of relationships in our lives. Hoarding, or hanging on to old personal belonging or items that are not being used, can make us stagnate and become toxic if we allow them to accumulate, leaving us feeling unwell.

Pre-Detoxification Checklist

- ✓ Choose organic food where possible. If not possible, choose fruits and vegetables that have the least exposure to chemicals, such as ones with skins that can be peeled. Products that are exposed, such as grapes, should be rinsed with apple cider vinegar and water before consumption.
- ✓ During the cooked food phase steam, sauté or braise your food, avoiding barbecuing or frying at high temperatures. Use stainless steel or iron; avoid Teflon or aluminium pots and pans.
- ✓ Avoid food and drinks that are packaged in plastic. Buy glass packages where possible.
- ✓ Drink two to three litres (eight to twelve cups) of clean, filtered water in glass containers only.
- ✓ Limit exposure to electromagnetic radiation: remove all electrical devices from your bedroom and place them in another room. Switch all power outlets off at the switch, especially while sleeping. Minimise the use of social media and television for the two weeks of your detox. Turn wifi networks off at the source.
- ✓ Replace all cleaning items such as laundry and household cleaning products and avoid using non-natural products. Replace with natural cleaning products, such as eucalyptus, bicarbonate soda (baking soda), or apple cider vinegar added to water to use as all-purpose cleaners.

✓ Flip through your cell phone address book and delete numbers of people who no longer serve you or lead to negative feelings when you think of them. Hanging on to contacts that no longer serve your purpose only weighs you down and holds you back from moving to where you want to be. For unhealthy relationships, use these fourteen days as an opportunity to consider any changes you can make.

✓ Clear out old clothes that are not being worn and gift them to a local church or thrift store in your area. These clothes sitting in your closet might be clutter and accumulation to you but cherished by someone else.

✓ Take the opportunity to consider removing any other items in your house that makes it feel toxic or cluttered. Not only will you feel lighter, you will set a great precedent for your physical detox.

✓ Ensure during your detox to breathe fresh air daily. Where possible go to the cleanest area you know and exercise.

✓ Utilise saunas or baths with Epsom salts, magnetic clay, or essential oils to help purge your body of toxins.

Fourteen-Day Kick-Start Breakthrough Cleanse

• Start on a day when you don't have to work hard or do anything strenuous to prevent tiredness. Start by cutting out alcohol, black tea, and coffee for the duration of the detoxification (fourteen days). Please note that you may experience headaches withdrawing from caffeine after approximately two or three days. (Optional: go to your local naturopath and request the following herbal detox tonic to be taken at 7.5 ml (1.5 teaspoons) per day for the duration of the detox.)

• **St. Mary's thistle, 60 ml.**

• **peppermint, 30 ml.**

• **turmeric, 60 ml.**

• **burdock root, 20 ml.**

• **dandelion root, 20 ml.**

• **green tea, 10 ml.**

- Day 1: Fasting: drink two to four litres (eight to 16 cups) of clean, filtered water and organic herbal tea only for this day (add lemon or a pinch of bicarbonate soda to your water). You may drink as much tea as you like for this day. Ensure teas selected are suitable for your blood type. Refer to your blood type list. For caffeine withdrawal drink organic green tea. This will supply you with clean caffeine along with your detox tonic. My suggestion for all blood types is to drink green, dandelion, liquorice, peppermint, rosemary teas.

- Days 2–3: Add freshly squeezed organic vegetable and fruit juice according to your blood type (see diet list according to blood type in the diet section). (Avoid large doses of spinach and kale if you have a history of kidney stones).

- Days 4–5: Eat only raw organic fruit and vegetables for your main meals three times a day. Along with this consume Clean Protein shakes (recipe follows) at the start and end of each day.

  (Please visit the resources section for where to purchase Clean Protein for all blood types).

Shake Recipe

1 scoop 100% Clean Rice Protein suitable for all blood types

1/2 cup berries or banana (depending on blood type)

300 millilitres (10 ounces) organic rice milk or almond milk

In a blender, combine all ingredients.

- Days 6-14: Add grilled white fish (one low on the food chain, such as sardines or mackerel with a fillet size of no more than thirty centimetres (twelve inches), and from clean waters such as Norway) according to your blood type. (Please see diet list in the next section.) Consume this with your vegetables for lunch and dinner. You may now have your protein shake as a meal for breakfast, afternoon or in the evening as a snack.

Caution

There are times we need to express caution when detoxing. For example, when your immune system is run down in a state of chronic fatigue, your body might not be able handle detoxification. Detoxing releases toxins and requires your immune system to be functioning well to facilitate removal of toxins. If your system is run down, go slow and easy. Start by doing only seven days if you're unable to handle fourteen. This may then be repeated at a later date as your body is able to handle it. This also applies to anyone with a debilitating illness. Go slow and easy. If you have concerns, please have your naturopath assess and monitor your progress.

Other times to express caution is if you are on prescription medication that is dependant on it being stored in the liver, such as antidepressants. Again, if you have concerns, please contact your physician.

Adopting the blood type diet recommended by this book will start a process of detoxification in your body, but for the majority of people I recommend starting with this program that you can easily do at home without any special detoxification supplements. (However, for additional benefits I recommend using the detox tonic given above.)

Step 3—The Nutrition and Dietary Plan

Eating the right diet should be an intuitive and automatic process, but due to rising obesity rates and chronic health conditions such as cancer and diabetes, this suggests that we're not eating according to our individual health requirements. Furthermore, there is a plethora of diets that can be utilised for this part of your program either on their own or in combination with the blood type diet. I want to start with a diet that will build the foundation from a genetic standpoint and build on that as you progress.

As discussed in the previous part of the book, we are all individuals and our blood type can give easy access and insight into our genetics and what diet and exercise plan is specifically suited to who we are and our needs for good health. This is where I want you to start. Following is a series of tables that show which foods are best suited to your blood type. During the next week of your plan, focus solely on eating according to your blood type. When this is part of your new life, we will move on to focusing on incorporating stress management and exercise while still continuing to follow the blood type diet.

For this part of the plan the type of food you eat is the focus. However, it's also important to be mindful of your macronutrient intake, such as protein, carbohydrates, and fats. Research shows that our digestive capabilities vary according to our blood type with some blood types more suited to a high protein diet and others to a more vegetarian style of diet. An example of this is the difference between blood types A and O. O type individuals have high levels of stomach acid for protein digestion, low levels of carbohydrate digesting enzymes called amylase, and high fat digesting enzymes called alkaline phosphatases, enabling them to eat a diet high in protein, low in carbs, and high in fat.

A types are at the opposite end of the spectrum and have low basal stomach acid levels, high amylase, and low levels of alkaline phosphatase. So naturally a diet that reflects their digestive capabilities is more geared toward a vegetarian/white meat diet. Refer to individual diet plans.

For the above reasons, portion control of protein-carbohydrates-fats varies according to each blood type, and this will help fine-tune your eating plan. The following four pie charts show a breakdown of the requirements for each blood type.

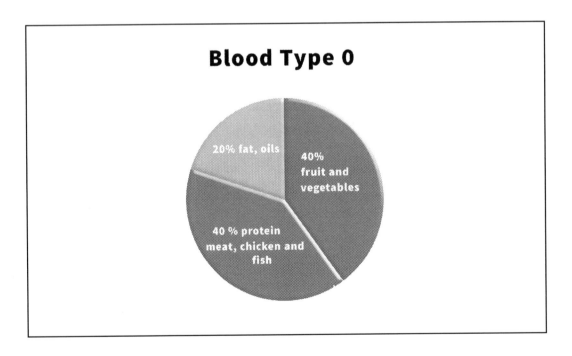

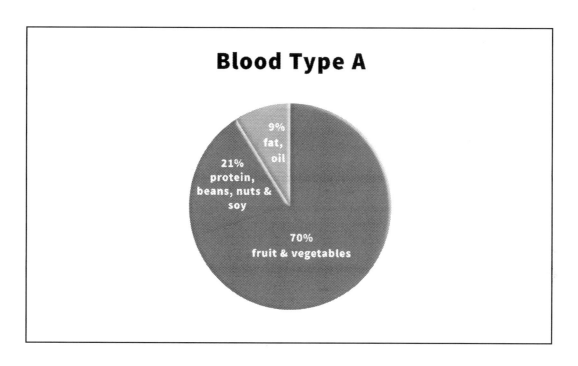

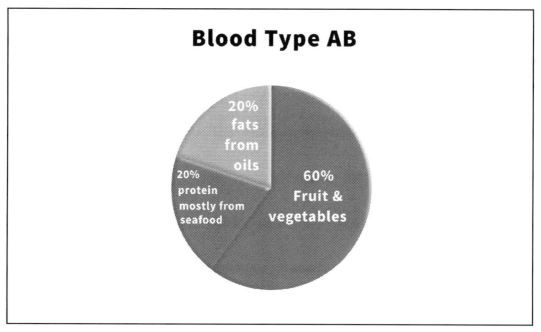

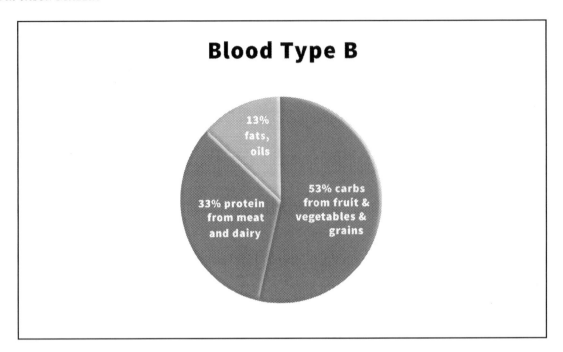

Blood Type B

13% fats, oils

33% protein from meat and dairy

53% carbs from fruit & vegetables & grains

To follow the diet plan, simply choose foods that are in the beneficial and neutral columns and avoid the ones in the avoid section. Remember to adjust your diet to the ratios that are more suitable for you. Don't worry if you happen to eat something in the avoid section, just get back to the beneficial and neutral next meal. Again, we're looking for progress, not perfection, so if you can follow a blood type diet at least 80 percent of the time, you will go a long way to feeling a lot better. Diet is one of your most important foundational rituals to make an automatic process, so implement this over the next seven days and continue as you progress through the program. Remember that further modifications to your diet can be made as your progress on your own or with the help of a clinician.

O Blood Type Eating Plan

Food Category	Beneficial	Neutral	Avoid
Meats	Beef, veal, lamb, veal, venison, hearts, buffalo, sweetbreads, mutton	Chicken, Cornish hens, duck, goat, goose, grouse, Guinea hen, horse, ostrich, partridge, pheasant, rabbit, squab, squirrel, turkey	Bacon, ham, pork, quail, turtle
Fish and Seafood	cod, perch, pike, bass, halibut, red snapper, shad, sole, sturgeon, swordfish, tilefish, trout, yellowtail	Anchovies, Beluga, bluefish, bullhead, butterfish, carp, caviar, chub, crab, clam, croakers, cusk, drum, eel, flounder gray sole, grouper, haddock, hake, halfmoon fish, harvest fish, herring, lobster, mackerel, mahi mahi, monkfish, mullet, mussels, opaleye, orange roughy, oyster, parrot fish, pickerel, pompano, porgy, rosefish, saltfish, salmon, sardine, scallop, scrod, scup, shark, shrimp, smelt, snail, sucker, sunfish, tilapia, trout, tuna, weakfish, whitefish, whiting	Abalone, barracuda, catfish, conch, frog, muskellunge, octopus, Pollack, squid

Dairy And Eggs		Duck egg, chicken egg farmer's cheese, feta, ghee (clarified butter), goat cheese, mozzarella, soy milk, rice milk	American cheese, blue cheese, brie, buttermilk, camembert, casein, cheddar, colby, cream cheese, edam, Emmenthal, gouda, gruyere, ice cream, Jarlsburg, kefir, cow's milk (all types), Monterey jack, muenster cheese, Neufchatel, paneer, parmesan, provolone, quark, ricotta, sour cream, string, Swiss, yogurt, goat's milk
Beans and Legumes	Adzuki beans, Black-eyed peas	Black bean, broad bean, cannelloni bean, fava bean, garbanzo, green beans, jicama, lima, mung Northern bean, snap bean, soybean, soy flakes, soy miso, soy tempeh, tofu, White bean	Kidney bean, lentils, red and green navy beans, pinto beans, tamarind bean
Nuts and Seeds	Pumpkin seeds, walnut, flaxseed	Almond, almond butter, almond cheese, almond milk, butternut, hazelnut, hickory, macadamia, pecan, pine nut, safflower seed, sesame seed, tahini	Beechnut, Brazil nut, cashew chestnut, peanuts, pistachios, poppy seeds

Grains and Starches	Essene bread	Amaranthe, artichoke pasta, buckwheat, Ezekiel bread, gluten free bread, kamut, millet, oat, flour, oat bran, oatmeal, quinoa, rice products, ryebread, rye flour, soba noodles, soy flour, spelt tapioca, teff	Barley, corn, cornmeal, couscous, gluten flour, popcorn, sorghum, wheat bran, wheat products, wheat germ, semolina, white flour
Vegetables	Beet greens, chicory, collard greens, dandelion, ginger, horseradish, kelp onions, seaweed, spinach artichokes, broccoli, escarole, kale, kohirabi, lettuce okra, parsnip, sweet potato, pumpkin, Swiss chard, turnip, garlic	Agar, arugula, asparagus, bamboo shoot, beet, Brussels sprouts, Chinese cabbage, cabbage juice, carrot, Celeriac, chervil, chilli pepper, cilantro, daikon radish, eggplant, endive, fennel, fiddlehead fern, garlic, mushroom abalone, enoki mushroom, matiake mushroom, oyster mushroom, portobello mushroom, straw mushroom, green olive, green pea, green pepper, pimento, poi, radichhio, radish, rappini, rutabaga, sauerkraut, scallion, senna, shallots, squash, tomato, water chestnut, watercress, yam, zucchini	Alfalfa, aloe, cauliflower, corn, cucumber, juniper, leek, mushrooms black olives, pickle, rhubarb, taro, yucca, acacia, caper, shitake mushroom, mustard greens, white potato.

Fruit and Fruit Juices	Banana, cherry, fifs, guava, mango, plums, prune, pineapple	Apple, Apple cider/apple juice, apricot, boysenberry, canag melen, casaba melon, Christmas melon, cranberry, Crenshaw melon, currants, dates, dewberry, elderberry, gooseberry, grape, grapefruit, kumquat, lemon, lime, loganberry, mulberry, musk melon, nectarine, ppaya, peach, pear, persimmon, pineapple, pomegranate, quince, raisin, raspberry, sago palm, Spanish melon, starfruit, strawberry, watermelon, youngberry	Asian pear, avocado, bitter melon, blackberry, cantaloupe, coconut milk, honey dew, kiwi, orange, tangerine, plantain

Oils	Flaxseed, olive	Almond, canola, cod liver, sesame, walnut	Castor oil, coconut, corn, cottonseed, peanut, safflower, soy, sunflower, wheat germ, evening primrose, blackcurrant seed oil, borage seed oil

| Herbs, Spices, and Condiments | Dulse, carob, curry, turmeric | Allspice, almond extract, anise, apple pectin, arrowroot, barley malt, basil, bay leaf, bergamot, caraway, cardamom, chilli powder, chives, chocolate, cinnamon, clove, coriander, cream of tarter, cumin, dill, gelatin, honey, liquorice, maple syrup, marjoram, mayonnaise, mint, molasses, mustard, oregano, paprika, peppercorn, peppermint, rice syrup, rosemary, saffron, sage, salad dressing, savoury, sea salt, soy sauce, spearmint, stevia, sucanat, brown, white sugar, tamarin, what free, tamarind, tarragon, thyme, vanilla, apple cider vinegar, wintergreen, Worcestershire sauce, brewers yeast | Blue-green algae, aspartame, carrageenan, corn syrup, cornstarch, dextrose, fructose, guar gum, guarana, ketchup, maltodextrin, MSG, black/white pepper, pickle, relish, vinegar, nutmeg |
| Beverages | Tea (green), seltzer water | Red wine | Coffee all types, liquor, soda, beer, tea, white wine |

A Blood Type

Food Category	Beneficial	Neutral	Avoid
Meats		Chicken, Cornish hens, grouse, Guinea hen, ostrich, squab, turkey	Bacon, buffalo, duck, goat, goose, ham, pork, turtle, horse, rabbit, beef, liver, lamb, veal, venison hearts, hearts, sweetbreads, mutton, squirrel, goat, partridge, pheasant, quail
Fish and Seafood	Mackerel, pickerel, pollack, salmon, sardine, snail, whitefish, carp, cod, whiting, monkfish, perch, trout	Abalone, bass, bullhead, butterfish, croaker, cusk, drum halfmoon, mahimahi, mullet, muskellunge, orange roughy, parrot fish, perch (ocean) perch (white)	Anchovies, crab, flounder, grey sole, grouper, haddock, hake, halibut, lobster, lox, octopus, scallop, shad, shrimp, sole, tilefish, barracuda, bass, beluga, bluefish, catfish, caviar, clam, conch, crab, eel, frog, harvest fish, herring (pickled and fresh) molluscs, opal eye fish, oyster, scup, squid

Dairy and Eggs		Duck egg, egg (chicken), egg white (chicken), egg yolk (chicken), farmer cheese, feta, ghee (clarified butter), goat cheese, goose egg, kefir, goats milk, mozzarella, paneer, quail egg, ricotta, salmon roe, sour cream (low- or non-fat), yoghurt	American cheese, blue cheese, brie, butter, buttermilk, camembert, casein, cheddar, colby, cream cheese, edam, Emmenthal, gouda, gruyere, ice- cream, Jarlsburg cheese, milk (cows, skim. or 2%), milk (cows whole), Monterey jack cheese, muenster cheese, Neufchatel, parmesan, provolone, Swiss
Beans and Legumes	Adzuki beans, black bean, black eyed peas, fava bean, lentil (domestic), lentil (red), miso, pinto bean, soy bean, soy flakes, soy granules, tempeh (fermented soy), tofu, green beans, soy cheese, soy milk	Broad bean, cannelloni bean, jicama, mung bean (sprouts), Northern bean, snap bean, white bean	Copper bean, garbanzo, kidney beans, lima bean, navy bean, red bean, tamarind bean

Nuts and Seeds	Flaxseed, walnut (black), walnut (English), peanut, peanut butter	Almond, almond butter, almond cheese, almond milk, beechnut, butternut, chestnut, hazelnut, hickory, litchi, macadamia, pecan, Pecan butter, Pine nut, Poppyseed, Safflower seed, Sesame butter (Tahini), Sesame seed, Sunflower butter, Sunflower seed	Brazil nut, cashew and cashew nut butter, pistachio
Grains And Starches	Amaranth, buckwheat/kasha, essene bread, oat flour, rice cake/flour, rye flour, soba noodles (100% buckwheat), soy flour bread, wheat bread (sprouted commercial), artichoke pasta	Wheat (whole wheat products), barley, corn (white, yellow, blue), cornmeal, couscous, Ezekiel bread, gluten flour, gluten free bread, kamut, millet, oat/oat bran/oatmeal, popcorn, quinoa, cream of rice, rice bran, rice (all forms), rice milk, wild rice, rye (100% rye bread), sorghum, spelt, spelt flour products, tapioca, wheat (gluten flour products), wheat (refined unbleached), wheat (semolina flour products), wheat (white flour products)	Teff, wheat (bran), wheat (germ)

Vegetables	Artichoke, beet greens, broccoli, carrot and carrot juice, celery and celery juice, chicory, collard greens, dandelion, fennel, garlic, ginger, horseradish, kale, kohlrabi, leek, lettuce (romaine), mushroom (silver dollar), okra, onion (green), parsnip, pumpkin, rappini, spinach and spinach juice, Swiss chard, turnip, alfalfa sprouts, aloe/aloe tea/aloe juice, escarole, mushroom (maitake), onion (red, Spanish, yellow)	Agar, arugula, asparagus, asparagus pea, bamboo shoot, beet, beet greens and juice, bok choy, Brussels sprout, cabbage juice, cauliflower, celeriac, chervil, cilantro, cucumber and cucumber juice, daikon radish, endive, fiddlehead fern, kelp, lettuce (bibb/Boston, iceberg, mesclun), mushroom (abalone), mushroom (oyster, enoki, Portobello), mushroom (straw), mustard greens, olive (green), oyster plant, pea (green/pod/ snow), pickle in brine, pimento, poi, radicchio, radish, radish sprouts, rutabaga, scallion, seaweed, senna, shallots, squash (summer/winter), string bean, taro, water chestnut, watercress, zucchini	Acacia (Arabic gum), potato (white/ red/blue/yellow), yucca, cabbage (Chinese, red, white), capers, chili pepper, eggplant, juniper, mushroom (shiitake), olive (black), olive (Greek/Spanish), pepper (green, yellow, jalapeno), pepper (red, cayenne), rhubarb, sauerkraut, sweet potato, tomato and tomato juice, yam

Fruit and Fruit Juices	Blackberry/blackberry juice, blueberry, cherry/ cherry juice, cranberry, figs (fresh, dried), grapefruit/ grapefruit juice, lemon/ lemon juice, pineapple/ pineapple juice, plum (dark/green/red), prune/ prune juice, water and lemon, apricot/apricot juice, boysenberry, lime/lime juice	Apple, apple cider/apple juice, avocado, breadfruit, canang melon, cantaloupe, casaba melon, Christmas melon, cranberry juice, crenshaw melon, currants (black/red), date, dewberry, elderberry(dark/ blue/purple), gooseberry, grape (black/concord/green/red), grape juice, guava/guava juice, kiwi, kumquat, loganberry, mulberry, musk melon, nectarine, nectarine juice, peach, pear/pear juice, Persian melon, persimmon, pomegranate, prickly pear, quince, raisin, raspberry, sago palm, Spanish melon, star fruit, strawberry, watermelon, youngberry	Banana, honeydew, orange/orange juice, plantain, coconut/ coconut milk, mango/ mango juice, papaya/ papaya juice, tangerine/tangerine juice
Oils	Flaxseed/linseed, olive, walnut, blackcurrant seed oil	Almond oil, borage seed oil, canola, cod liver, evening primrose oil, safflower, sesame, soy oil, sunflower, wheat germ oil	Castor oil, coconut, corn, cottonseed, peanut

Herbs, Spices, and Condiments	Barley malt, molasses, molasses (blackstrap), parsley, soy sauce, tamarin, turmeric, mustard (prepared vinegar free)	All spice, almond extract, anise, apple pectin, arrowroot, basil, bay leaf, bergamot, caraway, cardamom, carob, chives, chocolate, cinnamon, clove, coriander, corn syrup, cornstarch, cream of tartar, cumin, curry, dextrose, dill, dulse, fructose, guarana, honey, liquorice root, mace, maltodextrin, maple syrup, marjoram, mustard (prepared with vinegar), mustard (dry), nutmeg, oregano, paprika, peppermint, rice syrup, rosemary, saffron, sage, salad dressing, savoury, sea salt, spearmint, stevia, sugar (brown/ white), tamarind, tarragon, thyme, vanilla, yeast (bakers), yeast (brewers)	Chilli powder, guar gum, ketchup, mayonnaise, MSG, vinegar(all types), Worcestershire sauce, aspartame, Carrageenan, chilli powder, pepper (black/white), pepper (corn/red flakes), pickle relish, sucanat, wintergreen
Beverages	Tea (green), wine (red), coffee (regular/decaf)	Wine (white)	Liquor (distilled), seltzer water, soda (club), soda (all), tea (black, regular), beer

B Blood Type

Food Category	Beneficial	Neutral	Avoid
Meats	Goat, lamb, mutton, rabbit, venison	Beef, buffalo, liver (calves), ostrich, pheasant, turkey, veal	Chicken, Cornish hens, duck, partridge, quail, squirrel, bacon/ham/ pork, goose, grouse, guinea hen, heart, horse, squab, turtle
Fish and Seafood	Croaker, monkfish, perch(ocean), pickerel, sardine, caviar, cod, flounder, grouper, haddock, hake, halibut, harvest fish, mackerel, mahi mahi, pike, porgy, salmon, shad, sole, sturgeon	Abalone, bluefish, bullhead, carp, catfish, chub, cusk, drum, gray sole, halfmoon fish, herring/kippers(fresh), herring/ kippers(pickled), lox, mullet, muskellunge, opal eye fish, orange roughy, parrot fish, perch (silver/white/yellow), pompano, red snapper, rosefish, sailfish, scallop, scrod, scup, shark, smelt, squid, sucker, sunfish, swordfish, tilapia, tilefish, tuna, weakfish, whitefish, whiting	Anchovy, bass (bluegill/sea/striped), beluga, clam, conch, crab, eel, Japanese eel, frog, lobster, molluscs, mussels, octopus, oyster, pollack, shrimp, barracuda, butterfish, crab, snail (helix pomatia/ escargot), yellowtail

Dairy and Eggs	Farmer cheese, goat cheese, kefir, goat milk, mozzarella cheese, paneer, ricotta, cottage cheese, feta, cow milk (skim or 2%), cow milk (whole), yoghurt	Brie, butter, buttermilk, camembert, casein, cheddar, colby, cream cheese, edam, egg (chicken), egg white (chicken), egg yolk (chicken), Emmenthal cheese, ghee, gouda, gruyere, half and half, Jarlsburg, Monterey jack, Munster, Neufchatel, parmesan, provolone, quark, sherbet, sour cream (low-non fat), Swiss cheese, whey	Duck egg, goose egg, ice cream, quail egg, salmon roe, American cheese, blue cheese, string cheese
Beans and Legumes	Kidney, navy, lima	Broad bean, cannelloni bean, copper bean, fava bean, green bean, jicama, northern bean, red bean, snap bean, soy bean, tamarind bean, white bean	Adzuki, black bean, black-eyed pea, garbanzo, lentils (domestic/red/ green), Mung bean (sprouts), pinto, soy flakes, soy granules, soy(tempeh), soy (tofu), soy cheese, soy milk, soy (miso)
Nuts and Seeds	Walnut (black)	Almond/ almond (butter/cheese/ milk), beechnut, brazil nut, butternut, chestnut, flaxseed, hickory, litchi, macadamia, pecan/pecan butter, walnut (English)	Cashew/cashew butter, peanut/ peanut butter, pine nut, pistachio, poppy seed, pumpkin seed, safflower seed, sesame butter/ tahini, sesame seed, sunflower butter/ seed

Grains and Starches	Essene bread, millet, rice (puffed/rice bran), rice milk, rice cake/ flour, oat flour, oat/ oat bran/oatmeal, spelt	Barley, Ezekiel bread, gluten free bread, malt, quinoa, rice (cream of), rice (white/brown/ basmati) bread, soy flour bread, spelt flour products, wheat (refined/ unbleached), wheat (semolina flour products),wheat (white flour products), wheat bread (sprouted commercial—not Ezekiel)	Buckwheat/kasha, corn (white/yellow/ blue), cornmeal, kamut, popcorn, rye flour, rye/100% rye bread, soba noodles (100% buckwheat), sorghum, amaranth, artichoke pasta (pure), couscous (cracked wheat), gluten flour, wild rice, tapioca, teff, wheat (bran, germ), wheat (gluten flour products), wheat (whole wheat products)

| Vegetables | Beet, beet greens/juice, broccoli, Brussels sprouts, carrot, collard greens, ginger, kale, mushrooms (shiitake), mustard greens, parsnip, potato (sweet), cabbage (Chinese/red/white), cabbage juice, cauliflower, eggplant, pepper (green/yellow/jalapeno), pepper (red/cayenne), yam | Agar, alfalfa sprouts, arugula, asparagus, asparagus pea, bamboo shoots, bok choy, capers, carrot juice, celeriac, celery/celery juice, chervil, chicory, chili pepper, cilantro, cucumber/cucumber juice, daikon radish, dandelion, endive, escarole, fennel, fiddlehead fern, garlic, horseradish, kelp, kohlrabi, leek, lettuce (bibb/Boston/iceberg/mesclun), lettuce (romaine), mushroom (abalone), mushroom (silver dollar), mushroom (maitake), mushroom (oyster/enoki/portobello), mushroom (straw), okra, onion (green), onion (red/spanish/yellow), oyster plant, pea (green/pod/snow), pickle (in brine), pickle, pimento, poi, potato (white/red/blue/yellow), radicchio, rappini, rutabaga, sauerkraut, scallion, seaweed, senna, shallots, spinach/spinach juice, squash (summer/winter), string bean, Swiss chard, taro, turnip, water chestnut, watercress, yucca, zucchini | Acacia (Arabic gum), aloe/ aloetea/ aloe juice, olives (black), olives (greek/spanish), radish, radish sprouts, rhubarb tomato/tomato juice, artichoke (domestic/globe/jerusalem), juniper, olive (green), pumpkin, |

Fruit and Fruit Juices	Cranberry/cranberry juice, pineapple/ pineapple juice, plum (dark, green, red), watermelon, banana, grape (all types), papaya/papaya juice	Apple, apple cider/apple juice, Asian pear, blackberry/ blackberry juice, blueberry, boysenberry, bread fruit, canang melon, cherry (all), Christmas melon, currants (black, red), date, dewberry, elderberry (dark, blue, purple), fig (fresh, dried), gooseberry, grapefruit/ grapefruit juice, guava/guava juice, honeydew, kiwi, kumquat, lemon/lemon juice, lime/lime juice, loganberry, mango/mango juice, mulberry, musk melon, nectarine/nectarine juice, orange/ orange juice, peach, pear/pear juice, Persian melon, plantain, prune/prune juice, quince, raisin, raspberry, sago plum, Spanish melon, strawberry, tangerine/ tangerine juice, water and lemon, youngberry	Avocado, persimmon, pomegranate, coconut milk, prickly pear, star fruit
Oils	Olive oil	Almond, Blackcurrant seed oil, Cod liver, Evening primrose, Flaxseed (linseed), Walnut	Borage seed, Castor, Coconut, Corn, Cottonseed, Peanut, Safflower, Sesame, Soy, Sunflower, Canola

Herbs, Spices, and Condiments	Curry, liquorice root, blackstrap molasses, parsley	Anise, apple pectin, arrowroot, basil, bay leaf, bergamot, caraway, cardamom, carob, chilli powder, chives, chocolate, clove, coriander, cream of tartar, cumin, dill, dulse, fructose, honey, mace, maple syrup, marjoram, mayonnaise, mint, molasses, mustard(prepared, vinegar free), mustard (prepared with vinegar), mustard (dry), nutmeg, oregano, paprika, pepper (peppercorn/red pepper flakes), peppermint, pickle relish, rice syrup, rosemary, saffron, sage, salad dressing, savoury, sea salt, spearmint, sugar (brown/white), tamarin, tamarind, tarragon, thyme, turmeric, vanilla, vinegar (apple cider)	Almond extract, aspartame, Carrageenan, corn syrup, cornstarch, guar gum, ketchup, msg, pepper (black/white), allspice, barley malt, cinnamon, dextrose, gelatin plain, guarana, maltodextrin, soy sauce, stevia, Sucanat
Beverages	Tea (green)	Beer, coffee (regular/decaf), tea (black/regular/decaf), wine (red), wine (white)	Liquor (distilled), seltzer water, soda (club), soda (misc./ diet/cola)

AB Blood Type

Food Category	Beneficial	Neutral	Avoid
Meat and Poultry	Turkey	Lamb, mutton, rabbit	Bacon, ham, pork, chicken, Cornish hens, duck, grouse, guinea pig, horse, partridge, quail, squab, squirrel, turtle, beef, buffalo, goose, hearts/ sweetbreads, veal, venison
Fish and Seafood	Mackerel, mahi mahi, snail (helix pomatia/ escargot), tuna, cod, grouper, monkfish, pickerel, pike, porgy, sailfish, sturgeon	Abalone, bluefish, bullhead, butterfish, carp, catfish, caviar, chub, croaker, cusk, drum, halfmoonfish, harvest fish, herring, mullet, muskellunge, mussels, opal eye fish, orange roughy, parrot fish, perch (all types), pollack, pompano, rosefish, scallop, scrod, scup, shark, smelt, squid, sucker, sunfish, swordfish, tilapia, tilefish, weakfish, whitefish	Anchovy, barracuda, bass (all types), beluga, clam, conch, crab, eel, flounder, frog, haddock, hake, halibut, octopus, oyster, sole, trout (brook), trout (rainbow), trout (sea), whiting, yellowtail, whitefish

Dairy and Eggs	Egg white (chicken), goat cheese, kefir, mozzarella, ricotta, yoghurt, cottage cheese, farmer cheese, feta cheese, milk (goat), sour cream (low/ non fat)	Casein, cheddar, colby, cream cheese, edam, egg yolk (chicken), Emmenthal cheese, ghee (clarified butter), goose egg, gouda, gruyere, Jarlsburg, milk (cow-skim or 2%), Monterey jack cheese, muenster cheese, Neufchatel cheese, paneer, quail egg, quark cheese, string cheese, Swiss cheese, whey	Brie, duck egg, salmon roe, American cheese, blue cheese, butter, buttermilk, camembert, half & half, ice cream, milk (whole cow), parmesan, provolone
Beans and Legumes	Pinto beans, soy (miso), soy (tempeh), Navy bean, soybean, soy (tofu)	Broad beans, cannelloni beans, copper bean, green bean, jicama, lentil (domestic), lentil (red), northern bean, snap bean, soy cheese, soy flakes, soy granules, soy milk, tamarind bean, white bean	Adzuki beans, black beans, black eyed peas, fava beans, garbanzo beans, kidney beans, lima beans, mung beans (sprouts)
Nuts and Seeds	Peanut, peanut butter, walnut (black), walnut (English), chestnut	Almond, almond butter, almond cheese, almond milk, beechnut, brazil nut, butternut, cashew nut, cashew nut butter, flaxseed, hickory, litchi, macadamia, pecan, pecan butter, pine nut (pignola), pistachio, safflower seed	Hazelnut, poppy seed, pumpkin seed, sesame butter/tahini, sesame seeds

Grains and Starches	Amaranth, Essene bread, (manna bread), Ezekiel bread (commercial), millet, oat flour, oat/oat bran/ oatmeal, rice (puffed)/ rice bran, rice (white, brown, basmati) bread, rice (wild), rice cake/ flour, rice milk, rye flour, rye/100% rye bread, soy flour bread, spelt, wheat bread (sprouted commercial not Ezekiel)	Barley, couscous (cracked wheat), gluten flour, gluten free bread, quinoa, rice cream of, spelt flour products, wheat (bran), wheat (germ), wheat (gluten flour products), wheat (semolina flour products), wheat (white flour products), wheat (whole wheat products)	Artichoke pasta (pure), buckwheat/ kasha x, corn (yellow, white, blue), cornmeal x, popcorn, soba noodles (100% buckwheat), sorghum, tapioca, teff, kamut, wheat (refined unbleached)

Vegetables	Beet, beet greens, broccoli, cauliflower, collard greens, cucumber, dandelion, garlic, kale, mushroom (maitake), sweet potato, alfalfa sprouts, cabbage juice, carrot juice, celery/celery juice, eggplant, mustard greens, parsnip, yam	Agar, arugula, asparagus, bamboo shoot, bok choy, Brussels sprout, cabbage Chinese/red/white), carrot, celeriac, chervil, chicory, cilantro, cucumber juice, daikon radish, endive, escarole, fennel, fiddlehead fern, ginger, horseradish, juniper, kelp, kohlrabi, leek, lettuce (bibb/ Boston/iceberg/mesclun), lettuce (romaine), mushroom (silver dollar), mushroom (enoki), mushroom (straw), okra, olive (Greek/Spanish), olive (green), onion (all kinds), pea (green/ pod/snow), pimento, poi, potato (white, red, blue, yellow), pumpkin, radicchio, rappini, rutabaga, sauerkraut, scallion, seaweed, senna, shallots, spinach/spinach juice, squash (summer/winter), string bean, Swiss chard, taro, tomato/ tomato juice, turnip, water chestnut, watercress yucca, zucchini	Acacia (Arabic gum), aloe/aloe tea/aloe juice, artichoke(domestic/ globe/Jerusalem), olive (black), pepper (green/yellow/ jalapeño), radish, radish sprouts, rhubarb, caper, mushroom (shiitake), pepper (red/cayenne), pickle (in brine), pickle (in vinegar)

| Fruit and Fruit Juices | Cherry (all), cherry juice (black), fig (fresh/dried), grape (all types), grapefruit, kiwi, loganberry, pineapple, plum (dark/green/red), watermelon, cranberry, cranberry juice, gooseberry, blackberry, blackberry juice | Apple, apple cider, apple juice, apricot, apricot juice, Asian pear, blueberry, boysenberry, breadfruit, canang melon, cantaloupe, casaba melon, Christmas melon, crenshaw melon, currants (black/red), dates (all types) elderberry (dark/blue/purple), grapefruit juice, honeydew, kumquat, lime/lime juice, mulberry, musk melon, nectarine/ nectarine juice, papaya, peach, pear/pear juice, pineapple juice, plantain, prune/prune juice, raisin, raspberry, Spanish melon, strawberry, tangerine/tangerine juice, water and lemon, youngberry | Avocado, banana, bitter melon, dewberry, guava/guava juice, persimmon, pomegranate, prickly pear, quince, sago palm, coconut, mango/mango juice, orange/orange juice, star fruit (carambola) |
| Oils | Olive, Walnut | Almond oil, blackcurrant seed oil, borage seed oil, canola, castor, cod liver, evening primrose, flaxseed/linseed, peanut, soy, wheat germ | Corn, cottonseed, sesame, sunflower, coconut, safflower |

| Herbs, Spices, and Condiments | Curry, parsley | Apple pectin, arrowroot, basil, bay leaf, bergamot, caraway, cardamom, carob, chili powder, chives, chocolate, cinnamon, clove, coriander, cream of tartar, cumin, dill, dulse, honey, liquorice root, mace, maple syrup, marjoram, mayonnaise, molasses, mustard (prepared, vinegar free), mustard (dry), nutmeg, paprika, peppermint, rice syrup, rosemary, saffron, sage, savoury, sea salt, soy sauce, spearmint, stevia, sugar (brown/white), tamarin (wheat free), tamarind, tarragon, thyme, turmeric, vanilla, wintergreen, yeast (brewers) | Almond extract, Anise, aspartame, barley malt, Carrageenan, corn syrup, cornstarch, dextrose, fructose, gelatin plain, guar gum, guarana, ketchup, maltodextrin, pepper (white/black), pepper (peppercorn/red flakes), pickle relish, sucanat, vinegar (balsamic/cider/ red wine/ white/ rice), Worcestershire sauce, all spice, MSG |
| Beverages | Tea (green) | Beer, seltzer water, soda (club), wine (red), wine (white) | Liquor (distilled), coffee (regular/ decaf), soda (all), tea (black regular/decaf) |

Step 4—Stress Management and Exercise

For the next seven days you're going to focus on stress management and exercise and adding these to your existing routine. My first challenge for this week, along with the recommendations below, is to avoid all social media and television for seven days. While TV and social media can be positive, they are also a source of negative propaganda and stress for many individuals. Electromagnetic radiation can also be a stress factor, and many studies confirm their negative impact on our health and nervous systems. I strongly recommend doing this as it can have a profound affect on reducing your stress levels. It will free up more time to do the allocated tasks that are in alignment with your telos and allow the headspace for you to connect with yourself.

Regular exercise for at least thirty minutes per day (a minimum of four times per week) will ensure your body functions at an optimum level, which will assist you in various areas such as weight loss, reducing stress, and releasing endorphins. Along with diet, our blood type has a significant impact on what type of exercise is best suited to us, particularly with regard to managing stress. Your blood type is linked to fluctuating levels of the stress hormones and catecholamines (neurotransmitters) we produce and determines how we respond to stress and how quickly we recover from it.

Blood type A tends to be the most easily affected by stress, having the highest basal cortisol (stress hormone) levels. Meanwhile, type Os are at the opposite end of the spectrum from As with low basal cortisol and are the most stress resistant; however, when they're stressed, they have a harder time recovering. Blood type Bs and ABs are in between these extremes, with Bs being more A-like in their stress responses than ABs, who are more O-like in their responses.

See the following table for further details on your blood type, and choose exercises that are suited to you. You will need to exercise for a minimum of four times per week, so choosing more than one exercise is recommended.

Please note: If you have any pressing physical or structural issues such as spinal disease or a medical condition that may prevent you from doing any of the following exercises, consult with your health care practitioner to determine which activity is suitable for you.

Blood Type O	Blood Type A	Blood Types B and AB
• Produces the least amounts of cortisol in response to stress • Takes longer to initiate the stress response, but once initiated, takes longer to restore balance • Susceptible to prolonged stress or the build up of uncleared adrenaline—can lead to adrenal-neurological exhaustion	• Tends to overreact to even minor stress • Has increased cortisol in the blood to begin with • Produces more cortisol and adrenaline in response to stressors than other blood types	• Type B is closer to type A and type AB is closer to Type O • Both types tend to be more emotionally centred • They are far more sensitive to stress-related imbalances • They respond quickly to stress-reducing techniques
• Regular brisk exercise for type O is the key to better emotional balance (through a healthy chemical transport system) • Try intense physical exercise, such as aerobics, running, martial arts, and resistance training	• Be careful not to overtrain as this releases even more cortisol • Choose calming exercises like hatha yoga and tai chi • Use relaxation techniques like meditation and deep breathing	• Use visualization and relaxation techniques • Try to balance intense physical exercise with meditative relaxing exercise like yoga and stretching or exercise with a mental component like swimming, tennis, or hiking

• May need to consider learning anger management techniques • Try to minimize monotony. Break up your workday with physical activity—especially if your job is sedentary • Avoid MAO-inhibiting antidepressants • Stop smoking and avoid stimulants	• Avoid sleep deprivation; go to bed by eleven p.m. and sleep close to eight hours • Keep a regular schedule • Try natural light therapy in your workspace—especially first thing in the morning • Try a full day of solitude once a month	• Honour your circadian rhythms • Be sure to get enough sleep—try to retire by eleven p.m. and expose yourself to bright light in the morning • Minimize surprise and avoid rushing • Break up your workday with physical activity

Once you know what exercise is suited to your blood type, it's important to schedule it into your plan. Decide what exercise you are going to do and when you are going to do it. Learn ways to become accountable for doing this exercise, such as organising with a friend. Routine and accountability are two of the biggest factors for ensuring that you meet your exercise requirements, particularly in the early stages where the effort is more evident than the reward.

Changing Your Mode of Being (MOB) and Managing Stress

Even when you're eating well and exercising regularly, there will still be times when your head is not in the right place and you need to rely on quick, simple, and effective techniques to control and change the mode of your being. First and foremost it is important to stop and listen to your intuition and ask yourself: How do I feel? What do I need? What can I do? Perhaps a simple glass of water can make all the difference, or perhaps you have identified that its been a few days since you've had sun on your face. While these may seem obvious, the key here is to stay tuned in to your intuition and day-to-day needs. By attending to your MOB, you stay in control. I can assure you these small adjustments can make all the difference to the way you feel and will keep you on track.

Here are quick and effective ways to change your MOB.

MOB Game Changers

- If you are light-headed, have a headache, or lack focus, drink filtered water because this will ensure your body stays hydrated and maintains your level of clarity and concentration.

- If you're lacking nutrition, try a healthy snack, one high in protein and low in sugar, such as nuts. This will provide fuel for brain neurotransmitter production such as dopamine.

- Perhaps you feel irritable or stressed and non-productive. Try being mindful of your breath. Use a five second breathing in and out technique to calm your nervous system and increase blood flow to the brain. While closing your eyes, breathe in this manner continually for three to four minutes. You can do this at any time of the day. Also include a positive feeling such as gratitude, or visualise something you love in your life, such as your pet, a relative, a friend, or a place.

- Ask yourself what is one thing you are grateful for and then one thing that excites you. Spend thirty seconds focusing on each.

- Go for a quick walk in the sun, breathing fresh air as you walk.

- If you're home, take a warm bath, as this will invigorate your blood.

- If feeling tense, take a moment to stretch muscles that feel tight.

- If your job involves sitting for long periods of time and you're feeling tired and lacking energy, try standing up and sprinting on the spot for thirty seconds at any given time. This will jolt your nervous system and increase energy to your brain and provide you with clarity.

Nature provides the best cures. The six best "doctors" crucial in our well-being are fresh air, exercise, water, rest, good diet, and sunshine, so remember to include these when changing your mode of being.

Step 5—Mastering Your Mind-Set and Creating Your Life

You have completed a detox, implemented the blood-type diet, and learned how to mange stress and exercise. These components are now part of your every day life and provide and solid foundation. Now, with newfound clarity, you may be closer to understanding your telos, and it's time to start focusing on mastering your mind-set to achieve it. If you don't know this already then this section will guide you further toward it. Now add this part into your routine and focus on it for the next 7 days.

Part 1—Create a Clear Mode of Being and Find Your Telos

I want you to spend a minimum of ten minutes at the beginning of each day every day concentrating on breathing as a form of meditation, as this will help you tune in to your telos. This exercise can be done while stationary or walking mindfully.

To start, first relax. I want you to remove distractions from your mind by breathing in for five seconds and then out for five seconds. On the out breath, be mindful to breathe out any negative feelings. On the in breath think of something that gives you joy, and draw this feeling in as you breathe. Repeat this until you feel more clarity and calmness coming into your mind. This will regulate your heart and make it rhythmic, ensuring that it is pumping plenty of oxygen into the body and the brain. Mindful breathing is the simplest and quickest method you can use to get your body and mind connected and into a clearer mode of being. You can do this for as long as you like however to start, focus on doing this in every morning as this will set the tone for the day.

Now, listen to the peace and serenity, listen your heart in your calm state, and listen to questions in your mind during your current mode of being related to your telos. The important thing here is to answer truthfully if you are to come closer to your true path. Remember you can also do this process while mindfully walking or pacing.

Questions you may ask may include

- Why am I here?
- What are my highest values and priorities?
- How do I want to live my life?
- What is my purpose?
- If I die tomorrow, what would I regret not doing?
- As a child, what did I aspire to do or be?

- When I am in my element, what am I normally doing?

- If money wasn't a necessity, what would I do and aspire to be?

- What would I do every day for free?

- If I read my own obituary, how would it sound, and how would I want to be remembered?

- If I were to leave a legacy, what would that be?

Asking these questions and answering truthfully will help you to narrow down your telos; if it doesn't come right away, be patient. The fact that you want to know means it will come. Most importantly, ask the right questions, answer truthfully, remain open to the answers, and they will come. They may not come as you ask but may come in your day-to-day activities. Many of my answers came as messages in my dreams or from people in conversation. Much of this book came to me after asking related questions and waking up with the answers and inspiration to write in the early morning. Remember that when you ask the questions and decide you want to know something, your RAS will kick in and work full time to bring it into your consciousness.

If you have found your telos, these answers will excite you. They will make you want to get up in the morning and work toward making it your reality. Usually there will be many answers to these questions because there are many parts to your telos. For me, part of my telos is to travel the world inspiring, educating and helping people live amazing lives, to get as many people involved in healing as possible and to have a free healthcare retreat for the under privileged.

Once are clearer on your telos, visualise how it will make you feel once you have fulfilled it. Picture it in your mind. I see myself on a stage, giving a talk that inspires the audience. Or I visualise myself signing copies of this book for millions of people worldwide. I feel the warmth coming from patients when I help them take control of their health and happiness. You need to do the same thing for your telos. Feel it now. This will get you into the frequency of fulfilling your telos, even though you are not physically there yet.

Visualisation is important because when we do it, our RAS starts to associate with the things we need to create it. We become aware of opportunities that we otherwise would not have seen. Everything starts to come into your consciousness that is going to relate to you achieving your telos.

Part 2—The Happiness Project

There are more than 225 studies that study the benefits of happiness. Research by S. Lyubomirsky, L.A. King and E. Diener show that happy people

- are more productive and creative;
- make more money and have high-end jobs;
- are better leaders;
- are more likely to marry and less likely to divorce;
- have more friends and social support;
- have stronger immune systems and are healthier;
- are more likely to help others; and
- are more resilient when it comes to trauma and stress.

While achieving all of the above is desirable for many of us, I want to focus on creating happiness to help you create the life you want from this mode of being. This will be again important when you do the life creation ceremony in the next part.

There are many strategies you can use to make you feel happy and to master your state of mind. For the following task I have selected strategies that best suit this program and that are the most popular among past participants. Along with the first task I want you to choose from one of the following strategies and implement it over the course of the next seven days. Be sure to choose one task that you know you will be able to do every day and one that is the closest fit for you.

- **Gratitude Journal**: For seven days write seven things you're grateful for in your life. You may choose things that have recently happened, or from the past. For example, gratitude for your health now, for the information in this book, for feeling energised as a result, for the love of your family, for the companionship of a pet, or simply for the food you have to eat today. Perhaps you have been given a pay bonus at work. Be sure to be grateful as you journal.

- **Practice Acts of Kindness**: Every day, simply perform five acts of kindness to either a work colleague, friend, family member, or random person.

- **Goal and Telos Focus**: Every day take ten minutes to think about the very best possible life you could have for yourself in the future, the best career, your dream business or dream lifestyle. Think of the best possible version you can ever imagine of yourself. For fifteen minutes I want you to write down what you imagined. Draw pictures if you need to be graphic.

Part 3—The Life Creation Ceremony

I recommend that all my clients create a vision of what they want to create in their lives for the next five years. There are three steps to this process:

Brainstorming

Set aside a day on your calendar for what I call a life creation ceremony. Normally I prefer people choose a day that has great significance such as a birthday, a day of triumph, or a day when you achieved success in your life. As we are doing this as part of this program, choose a day of the week that is your favourite relaxed day such as a Sunday. If you choose a day that means something to you, it will add more power to this process. (Remember, you can always do this part of the program at a later date if you wish.) Personally I choose days that have the number eleven as this is a power number for me. As the title *The Wounded Healer* suggests, you're going to create your life, the life you want. I call this a ceremony as we need to make an event that we remember and put time and energy into the process. In putting energy into this process, the possibility of manifestation becomes even greater. Let me ask: Have you ever not gotten something out of something you put immense energy into? The life creation ceremony can be done alone, with a friend, or with a partner. I recommend for your first one to do it alone. Then you may do a joint one with your life partner.

I want you to choose a special place you love, such as a power spot or a place in nature with your favourite view. Rid yourself of any distractions and become present as to where you are as to make it more memorable. Breathe slowly using the given method in **Part 1—Create a Clear Mode of Being and Find Your Telos.**

Now tune in to your telos and purpose, and reflect on the life you want and what you see yourself doing now and in the next five years. Next, on a piece of paper, start *quickly* writing down any ideas that come to you connected to your dreams and desires. I want you to think of the following areas:

➢ money and finance;

➢ relationships and love;

➢ career or vocation;

➢ lifestyle, travel, and leisure;

➢ health, and personal and spiritual development; and

➢ philanthropy, charity, and legacy

The true answers about what you want are in your subconscious mind, not your conscious mind. I want you to remember to do this task quickly and allow anything to come to you from your subconscious mind without over-thinking it. Spend five to ten minutes writing down everything that comes to you for each category. I now want you to stop and look at what you have written and select the things that first jump out at you from each category and list them corresponding to the above categories. It's acceptable if you don't have something for every category. Some things may be added later. The first part of the task is now complete. Spend some time now enjoying the place you love for the rest of the day and make it a memorable one!

Timeline and Goal Setting

I want you to do the same as brainstorming for this next part. Again pick a day of significance and go to your special place. Get yourself in a great mode of being through selecting nice environment and clear your mind of distraction. By this stage you would have narrowed down what you would like to achieve for each category. Reflect on what you have selected and ask yourself: If I had only five years to achieve my goals when would I like to achieve each goal by? What goal can I achieve reasonably quickly and which goals will take time? What is my first step and what action do I need to take immediately to start the process of achieving each goal? Remember we are looking for progress not perfection here. Start with the start date for each steps and a completion date.

When creating your goals be specific and realistic. Set a time frame for achieving each goal and note the steps that are required to move you toward achieving it.

When deciding on your goals, it is important to have at least 80 percent belief that they are possible to achieve. There's no point thinking you are going to climb Mount Everest within three months if you have never even done any mountain climbing training. That doesn't mean climbing Mount Everest can't be a long-term goal, but it will be necessary to establish short-terms goals leading toward it first.

Here's an example of the life creation timeline table you can use as a template.

Life creation timeline table

Life Area	Goal	Action steps now	Action steps date	Final date of manifestation
Health, Personal/ Spiritual	Lose 10 kgs	Make appointment with naturopath.	11/1/2015	Dec 2015
Career/Vocation	Start up my online business	Set up Facebook page, register business.	11/2/2015	Dec 2015
Relationship/Love	Meet the love of my life	Start going out more, register for online dating.	14/2/2015	Dec 2016
Lifestyle/Travel Leisure	Climb Mount Everest	Start hiking, call hiking group.	12/07/2015	June 2019
Money/ Finances	Make my first million	Join property investment group.	15/4/2015	June 2018
Charity, Legacy/ Philanthropy	Set up schools in third world country	Start making enquiries of costs. Research online.	14/4/2015	June 2020

Life Creation Board Ceremony

Finally, using your goal creation timeline table (as above), it's time to get into the creative process. I want you to first buy a large picture frame, about 300 millimeters x 450 millimeters (twelve to fifteen inches), with six sections for photo insertions (one for each part of your life). Next, flip through magazines or search the Internet for images that reflect the goals you want to achieve. Cut out or print at least three or four images that you connect with for each area. I want you to select images that jump out and most reflect your ultimate goals in all areas. If it's a particular car you want to buy, make sure it's the right model and colour you desire. Be very specific! Be sure to select images of things you see yourself doing make it very real and when you look at the picture make sure you can imagine what it would be like to be there already.

On my current vision board, in the career section I have picture of a speaker in front of a large audience. This connects with my desire to inspire people to live healthy and fulfilling lives. To reinforce the feeling of success, in the lifestyle section area I use the image of a new luxury car. I have images that symbolise the abundance that I want to receive, the type of house and location I want to live in, and the places I want to visit. Find images that resonate with your ultimate dreams. Label each section with the headings of the six areas—health-wealth-career-love, and so on. Sort out your images and then paste them in their correct section. Be sure to put the time and energy into creating it. The final most important thing to do is hang the picture frame on a wall where you can see it in your bedroom. Sleeping next to it every night will ensure you pick up its essence by osmosis taking it into your subconscious mind.

Look at this every morning and visualise how you will feel fulfilling your telos. Visualise yourself achieving your goals. When I look at my vision board every morning, I feel myself driving that car, sailing the yacht, and giving a keynote presentation. This will help connect you to fulfilling your telos and will help make achieving your goals a reality.

Some people underestimate the importance of visualisation, but there is a science to it. In the lead up to the 1980 Winter Olympics, Soviet scientists split a number of world-class athletes up into four groups. The first completed 100 percent physical training, the second 75 percent physical training and 25 percent mental training, the third 50–50, and the final group 25–75 percent. In subsequent testing the last group performed best, followed by the third, second, and first group, in that order. Once you begin using visualisation, you will realise its power.

Part 4—Visualisation and Affirmation

After compiling your life creation board, for each of the categories you will create an affirmation to say to yourself every morning when you arise. An affirmation is a visualisation that is tied to a specific goal. Its purpose is to get you to put yourself in the position of having achieved that goal already and to know how it would feel. For example, if one of your health goals is to lose ten kilograms so that you look good and feel energetic, then an affirmation you could say for that goal would be: "I am happy that I have lost ten kilograms and look good and feel energetic." Actually put yourself in that position. Feel yourself lighter. Feel yourself springing out of bed in the morning because you have more energy. Feel yourself wearing nice clothes that haven't fit you for years.

Create affirmations for all your overall life goals and write them down. Place them next to your vision board and say them daily. Use these as inspiration every morning to start your day.

Once you have completed your affirmations, take a moment to be thankful for what you already have. Gratitude is one of the most underrated keys to happiness. Unfortunately, a side effect of being focused on achieving goals is that we can spend so much time thinking about the future that we don't realise how truly blessed we are in the present moment. Some aspects of your life may not be perfect, but there are always things to be thankful for. For instance, the roof over your head, the food that nourishes your body and the warm rays of sunshine. Taking time to express gratitude on a daily basis will help you be happy now. You don't need to create a list for this aspect of the plan, just take a moment after your affirmations to think of all you have to be thankful for. Give gratitude for at least three aspects in your life that you're grateful for on a daily basis.

Your affirmations and gratitudes are the foundations of having the right mind-set to fulfil your telos. In addition to focusing on them as part of your daily ritual, the first thing I recommend saying every day is, "My life is amazing. I love my life. I am blessed."

Step 6—Loving Relationships

Your mind and body will be in the right place to start reaping the benefits of your hard work. Now we are going to focus on the area of relationships. Having a loving relationship with yourself and others has an enormous impact on our happiness and fulfilment.

If there is one relationship that can have more impact upon your being than any other, it is your personal intimate relationship that you may have with your life partner. So I am going to ask you to focus on this section for the next seven days. If you are not currently relationship you can still use this section to help you understand and improve your behaviour in relationships and use the action strategy when you do meet that special someone.

I have developed the seven keys for intimate relationships. The seven keys will help you nurture those relationships and to enable you associate them as having a positive impact in your life and to fulfil you in your telos.

The seven keys are

1. **Look After and Love Yourself**. If you're not taking care of and loving yourself, then you are not in a position to love someone else. Remember to fall back on yourself. Love and look after your own mental, spiritual, emotional and physical health. No one is going to do this for you. When issues arise, it's often our outlook on the situation that needs to change. Looking after yourself will give you clarity and self understanding and this will help you to deal with any difficult situations. Remember to go back to your foundations, good diet, exercise and change your mode of being. If you're having difficulty with any relationship take a step back and ask yourself, with new found clarity you can approach further discussions from a higher mode of being and from a place of love.

2. **Intimacy**. Allow yourself to be vulnerable to the other person. Catch yourself if you hide behind walls, and allow yourself to be seen. This will allow your partner to connect with you and see who you truly are. Make intimacy an everyday activity.

3. **Have a Retreat Space**. Relationships can face difficulties. Choose a place together where you are able to regroup and reconnect, whether it be at the beach or in bed. This

is a place where you can discuss new strategies for your relationship together. Ensure your retreat space automatically helps you both go in to your highest mode of being.

4. **Support Their Telos and Your Own Purpose.** It is essential to give your partner the space he or she needs to be able to follow passions and dreams so your partner can grow. Love and support you partner in the process of doing that. This means understand his or her telos, and support this person's quest—remember to come back to yourself and honour your own. This will ensure that you both honour your own journey and each other's.

5. **Communication.** Be clear about what you want and communicate it with your partner. Listen to what your partner wants until you both understand each other. Listen until you can see things from the other's perspective.

6. **Argue Fairly from a Space of Love.** Arguments are a normal part of relationships and can help us form new meanings around a given situation. They can assist our own growth and the growth of our relationships. There is, however, a significant difference between a healthy and unhealthy conflict. Address the issue at hand only. Direct any frustrations away from your partner and making it about them personally. Ensure you look at the behaviour rather than attack the person.

7. **Express Gratitude.** Make sure your partner understands how grateful you are for him or her and express it daily.

The Six Elements of Loving Relationships

For the next seven days you will need to focus on implementing daily actions to empower your intimate relationship. The next diagram highlights daily tasks that you will need to do to nurture your relationship. It is important to perform all tasks daily to get the most out of this exercise.

To begin, it's important to know which element is most important to your partner. Start by asking your partner to list the elements in the order of importance and do the same in return. Once you both have clarity on this, start listing next to each element an example of what you might like to do for each. For example, if your partner listed that "quality moments" is of utmost importance, think of ways you can satisfy this element. As listed below, perhaps taking a daily walk with your partner is a way to spend quality moments. Remember what you do to satisfy any given element may change as long the element is satisfied. For example, for quality moments you might go for a walk one day and perhaps spend time watching a movie the next day. Both are ways to satisfy one element.

For seven days I want you to do something for one other for each element. Once you have completed the seven days, continue with the elements that are most important to each person.

Quality Moments
eg. take a daily walk together.

Embrace
eg. hold hands or spend time holding each other.

Be of assistance
eg. make dinner for the other person.

Gifts
eg. pick a flower or buy some chocolate.

Praise and affirm
eg. tell him or her they are awesome at something.

Life creation
eg. dream and create your future together.

Once you have implemented these daily actions, you will soon start noticing how your partner responds to them. Given you have done this exercise correctly you will start to notice a positive change that will continue to help your relationship over time. Remember to check in with your partner regularly to ensure you're both up to date with each other's needs.

Step 7—Spiritual and Self-Development

Just hearing the word spirituality can be a challenge for some so rest assured the intention in this book is to honour your own belief. When I talk about spirituality, I am referring to *any* practice that connects you to your higher spirit mode, helps you to be in a state of peace, and connects you to yourself, the universe, or god. For some, going to a place of worship connects them, for others taking time out and visiting nature connects them, while practices such as yoga, Thai chi, and meditation works for many. In this section, if you have a spiritual practice, I want you to integrate it into your existing plan and practise this along with all the other elements you have now implemented.

If you don't already have a spiritual practice, here are some things you can consider. First ask yourself:

- What is spirituality to me?
- When am I most at peace and feel connected to my higher self?
- What do I believe in?
- What do I connect with?
- What books can I read to expand my knowledge of spirituality?

Find something that helps you to feel like you connect with yourself. For me, I find a nice walk in nature or by the sea connects me. For others it could be surfing, reading a book, sitting in a quiet room—something that's going to align you with your higher self. For the last seven days I want you to focus on adding this final element into your regime to complete the program.

Chapter 12

Getting It Done

Congratulations! You have now have completed the seven-step breakthrough to mastering your life and ultimate success. If you have followed the steps and implemented the strategies you will be well on the road to mastering your life.

You have implemented the following:

- completed a detoxification and gained clarity;
- introduced a blood type specific diet;
- implemented a blood type specific exercise and stress management;
- clarified your telos, set goals and created the life creation board;
- enhanced your relationships; and
- made time for and built awareness of your spirituality.

It's time to make it part of your everyday life and make it a mind-set. The key to the continued success of any plan is implementation and keeping yourself accountable. Let's again score ourselves out of ten in each of the areas of the six pillars of health and wellness using the following table.

Did you score higher? If so, which area has improved? If you scored higher, congratulations! Give yourself a huge pat on the back: boom, *progress*! Which area do you need to improve in? Now it's time to add a little more focus in this area as you progress and continue. What resources do you need to go to the next level? How do you feel and look? Are you more connected to your telos?

From this new headspace let's recreate an ongoing daily checklist that includes everything that you have implemented to propel you further forward. I want you to look toward a further vision of your best self. Tick off your checklist day by day as you continue to complete the given tasks. Not only will this list remind you of what step you need to be taking, it will also help you to keep yourself accountable and reinforce your tasks. If you miss checking off some of your rituals one day it's all right. To avoid compounding the problem, relax and start again. It can happen that you may miss some rituals and then lose sight of your telos and then suddenly you may lose your motivation and you miss more rituals. To avoid this happening to you, just stop, relax and start again. Pat yourself on the back for the good things you have done. You will be surprised how much you have achieved, even if you have missed some rituals. I often have clients coming in feeling like they have blown their plan because they have only kept to 90 percent of the blood type diet. I remind them that 90 percent is excellent. Being slack one day is no reason to give up. Be kind to yourself. If you've done the wrong thing today, just get back on track. Get it right from your next meal onwards.

If keeping yourself accountable is not something that comes easily to you, having the visual aid of the checklist could be enough to help you develop the habit. Many people also seek the help of a professional to hold them accountable. Whichever works for you, remember that this is meant to be fun. Our daily rituals are what give us the life we want. Regularly take time to reflect on your daily rituals to confirm that they are in line with your highest values.

Staying on Track and Motivated

The challenge facing everyone is to stay motivated. In the short term it will always be easier to do nothing than to push yourself. But with that choice you are also choosing to give up on your telos and choosing to give up on your goals. For some people the only thing that finally motivates them to get in control of their health and happiness is when they get sick, or a relationship fails, or something else in their life makes it clear that it is time for a change. I want you to be proactive, looking forward to your goals not back to your issues and to make living a healthy and happy life a priority for yourself. You now have the tools to live that life. Accept nothing but success and the amazing life you will have!

Sometimes you know what you want to achieve and you know what you need to do, but what you need is the energy to go and do it. Look at your life and see where your energy is being taxed. See if you can pull back from some of those things. Getting your health and happiness in order will ultimately give you more energy so you can contribute back to the world.

If you start implementing your plan but find that you have stopped two weeks later, ask yourself what happened. Figure out what you can change so that it doesn't happen again. Visualise how it will feel to be connected to your telos. Imagine how it will feel to achieve your goals. Connect to the energy of that. Use that as your daily motivation to keep going.

Think of your goals and ask yourself:

- Do I really want it?
- Why do I want it?
- How much do I want it?
- Where do I see myself in ten years if I keep going, and where will I be if I give up?
- Where are my current habits leading me and is that where I want to go?

At the end of the day I can't make you take action. You are the one who has got to do it. You have to stay self-motivated. You have to find what motivates you. That is the key. To break negative patterns and habits and to create new positive ones, takes around thirty days. Stick with all the components beyond the 8 week program and make it a part of your everyday life.

If people are not progressing in their lives, there's usually some major obstacle blocking them. That's why we call it a breakthrough when they overcome it. When you break that cycle of something that's affecting your life, you will feel liberated and can move on to the next stage of your life. For one person it might be a bad relationship, for another it might be a bad habit they picked up from their father like going straight to the pub after work and for some it might be a mental thought that they are not good enough. Whatever it is, you can begin turning your life around now. You will achieve health and happiness if you stick with it.

The Wounded Healer in You!

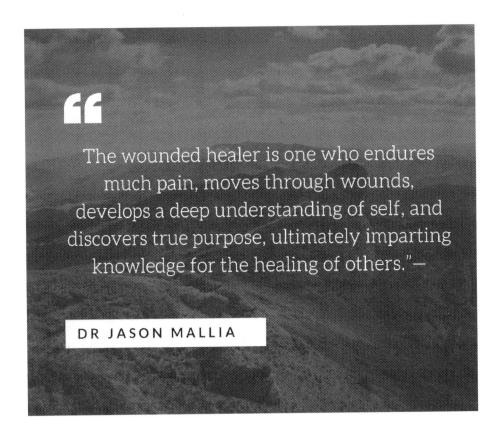

"The wounded healer is one who endures much pain, moves through wounds, develops a deep understanding of self, and discovers true purpose, ultimately imparting knowledge for the healing of others."—

DR JASON MALLIA

The Wounded Healer refers to the archetype created by Carl Jung, who described wounded healers as those who have gained pearls of wisdom after having risen from the depths of despair and times of darkness. I believe there is a wounded healer in all of us. Like my story, many of you have been wounded and have suffered to the point of breaking. However, we truly evolve when we come to realise that our pain carries a profound meaning and we can utilise our pain to understand ourselves and help others in the process. The archetype of the wounded healer reveals to us that it is only by being willing to face consciously the experience and move through our wounds, do we receive the blessing of being able to transcend and be of service to ourselves and others. It becomes our gift once we accept this as our journey.

In essence, when we accept and embrace our wounds in this way, the wound actually leads us to a deeper sense of self and moves us toward growth. The wounds take the function of helping us through the process of letting go of our old self and being recreated in the process. The wounds are not a static representation of who you are but rather a continuous evolutionary process that unfolds as we evolve ultimately connecting to our deeper sense of who we are.

As we face our experience, evolve, and transcend, the old self falls away, allowing the new self to move now from a new space. Many choose to remain stuck in their wounds instead of seeing the wounds as an opportunity to grow, often anchoring the pain with our grief and negative attachment to the pain. The key is to create a new meaning around your wounds and to look toward the new desired result once we discover what this is for you. For some, being wounded is the way they connect to their higher self-guiding them to a great sense of purpose.

Final Note and Resources

This book is designed as an education tool to propel you on your path to health, wellness, and living a life of purpose. I deeply respect and understand that many people have a wide variety of needs and are in different stages of their health and personal development. For some, this is a reminder of important messages to aid their journey while for others it's a starting point of self discovery. This is not intended to diagnose or act as a cure and no claims are made in this book to that conclusion. From my twenty years of clinical experience, I also understand that due to our individuality some may need further assistance depending on their blocks or challenges. Some may need medical assistance, or may need the help of an integrative medical practitioner to help them progress. For those wishing to develop further, the following resources are recommended.

Resources

For online self-help training courses, webinars, workshops, and public speaking engagements, visit the following website:

www.the-woundedhealer.com.

For the management of chronic medical conditions and for consultations and online Skype sessions:

www.integratedhealth.com.au.

For blood typing kits:

www.integratedhealth.com.au/shop/original-home-blood-typing-kit.

For assistance on genetic testing:

www.integratedhealth.com.au/shop/comprehensive-gene-testing.

To purchase blood type specific Clean Protein:

www.integratedhealth.com.au/shop/.

Other publications:

Mallia, Dr. Jason. *Concepts of Integrative Medicine,* edition 1. Sydney, NSW, Bookpal, 2012

www.amazon.com/Concepts-Integrative-Medicine-Jason-Mallia-ebook/dp/B00DNQ0P12

Integrated Health and Wellness Clinic Practice Australia

48 Norton St Leichhardt 2040 Sydney NSW Australia

Appendix

Integrated Health Evaluation Questionnaire

Welcome to your health evaluation questionnaire, which is designed to help you further understand yourself and give you a baseline of your current health status. Please complete this health evaluation at the beginning and end of your seven-step breakthrough program. You can use it any time you feel you need to track you progress and to stay on your path to optimum health and wellness. Please ensure you answer all questions in order to have an accurate representation of your health status. Be honest and be true to yourself.

Here's how it works.

Simply tick the number in the column which best describes the frequency or severity of your symptoms (0=low to 3=high) applying it to your previous month. Also circle the yes or no answers and apply the three points if you circle yes. Once you have completed the questions tally up your scores. The highest scores reflect the area(s) that require most attention. Should you be concerned about any of the results please contact your GP or naturopathic physician before commencing the program.

Note: This health evaluation does not aim to diagnose or replace a healthcare professional. It is a comprehensive guide and tracking tool for use with your program.

Section 1: Gastrointestinal System

Stomach Low acid	0	1	2	3
Indigestion				
Excessive belching, burping				
Bloating or fullness commencing during or shortly after a meal				
Sensation of food sitting in stomach for a prolonged period after a meal				
Bad breath				
Loss of appetite, or nausea				
History of anaemia N Y (3)				
TOTAL				

Hyper Acid Stomach	0	1	2	3
Stomach pain, burning or aching, 1-4 hours after eating				
Feeling hungry just an hour or two after eating				
Indigestion or heartburn from spicy or fatty food, citrus, alcohol, or caffeine				
Stomach discomfort or pain in response to strong emotions, thoughts, or smell of food				
Heartburn aggravated by lying down or bending forward				
Antacids, carbonated beverages, milk, cream or food relieve the above symptoms				
Constipation				
Difficulty or pain when swallowing				
Black tarry stools				
Vomiting blood or vomitus has appearance of coffee-grounds				
TOTAL				

Small Intestine/Pancreas	0	1	2	3
Indigestion, bloating and fullness for several hours after eating				
Abdominal cramps or aches				
Nausea and/or vomiting				
Excessive passage of gas				
Diarrhoea (loose, watery or frequent bowel movements)				
Constipation (requiring straining, or a hard, dry or small stool) Alternating constipation and diarrhoea				
Undigested food in stools				
Stools greasy, smelly or stick to toilet bowl				
Black tarry stools				
Certain foods worsen abdominal symptoms N Y (3)				
Dry flaky skin and dry brittle hair N Y (3)				
Difficulty gaining weight N Y (3)				
TOTAL				

Colon	0	1	2	3
Lower abdominal pain, cramping and/or spasms				
Lower abdominal pain relieved by passing gas or stool				
Excessive gas and bloating				
Certain foods or stress aggravate lower abdominal pain				
Diarrhoea (loose, watery or frequent bowel movements)				
Constipation (requiring straining, or a hard, dry or small stool)				
Alternating diarrhoea and constipation				
Sensation of incomplete emptying of bowel				
Extremely narrow stools				
Mucus or pus in stool				
Red blood with bowel movement				
Rectal pain or cramps				
Anal itching				
TOTAL				

Liver/Gallbladder/Pancreas	0	1	2	3
Upper abdominal pain, or pain under ribs				
Bloating or feeling of fullness after eating				
Excessive belching or gas				
Fatty foods cause indigestion or nausea				
Loss of appetite				
Nausea and/or vomiting				
Unexplained itchy skin				
Yellowish discolouration of skin or eyes, or dark coloured urine N Y (3)				
Pale clay-coloured stools				
Fatigue, malaise or weakness				
Fluid retention, oedema				
Easy bruising, or bleeding (e.g. of gums)				
Loss or thinning of body hair N Y (3)				
Red skin, particularly on palms N Y (3)				
Dry, flaky skin, or dry hair N Y (3)				
TOTAL				

Section 2: Hormones

Symptoms of underactive thyroid	0	1	2	3
Fatigue, sluggishness				
Feeling cold, or intolerance to cold				
Swelling or tightness in front of neck N Y (3)				
Constipation (requiring straining, or a hard, dry or small stool)				
Dry skin and hair N Y (3)				
Puffy face, hands or feet				
Gaining of weight, or decreased appetite N Y (3)				
Low mood				
Difficulty concentrating, poor memory				
Low libido				
Infertility N Y (3)				
Heavier or more frequent menstrual periods N Y (3)				
TOTAL				

Symptoms of overactive thyroid	0	1	2	3
Fatigue, notable weakness in limbs				
Feeling hot, or intolerance to heat, sweaty				
Swelling or tightness in front of neck N Y (3)				
Diarrhoea (loose, watery or frequent bowel movements)				
Weight loss, possibly with increased appetite N Y (3)				
Palpitations				
Nervousness, irritability, restlessness				
Tremor				
Insomnia				
Visual disturbance, problems with eyes, or development of staring gaze				
Poor libido				
Light, infrequent or absent menstrual periods N Y (3)				
TOTAL				

Stress, fatigue and adrenals	0	1	2	3
Feeling stressed, nervous, or tense, or unable to relax				
Feeling irritable or oversensitive				
Feeling overwhelmed, unable to cope				
Low mood, mood swings				
Difficulty concentrating or thinking clearly, memory problems				
Need coffee, tea, tobacco, sugar or chocolate as pick me ups				
Fatigued, tire easily				
Find it hard to get up and going in the morning				
Difficulty staying awake during day				
Insomnia				
Palpitations or chest pain				
Nausea, dizziness				
Change in appetite				
TOTAL				

Section 3: Immune

Low immunity	0	1	2	3
Frequent colds or flu N Y (3)				
Frequent infections in other locations (e.g. bladder, skin)				
Diarrhoea (loose, watery or frequent bowel movements)				
Ears continuously drain				
Nasal congestion or discharge				
Sore throat				
Cough with mucus				
Cold sores				
Inflamed or bleeding gums, or swollen, red lips or tongue				
Wounds heal slowly N Y (3)				
Excessive loss of hair N Y (3)				
Neck, armpit or groin swelling				
TOTAL				

Allergy	0	1	2	3
Migraine or non-migraine headache				
Sensitivity to light (skin or eyes)				
Dark circles under eyes				
Swollen eyes, lips, face, or other body parts				
Localised or general itching—eyes, ears, throat, nose, skin				
Rashes or eczema				
Clear watery discharge from nose or eyes				
Sneezing, coughing or wheezing				
Irritability, fatigue				
Certain foods worsen symptoms, or cause palpitations N Y (3)				
TOTAL				

Section 4: Detoxification

Detox	0	1	2	3
As far as you are aware, do you have a sensitivity or allergy to: The preservatives sodium benzoate or potassium benzoate Tyramine (red wine, cheese, bananas, chocolate) Caffeine Chemicals such as fragrances, exhaust fumes, cigarette smoke or other strong odours Even small amounts of alcohol Do you have a history of exposure to chemicals such as herbicides, insecticides, pesticides or organic solvents? N Y (3) Alcohol (number of drinks per week) 0, 1-7, 8-14, 15+ (1) (2) (3) Coffee or other caffeinated 0, 1-2, 3-4, 5+ drinks (number per day) (1) (2) (3) Smoking N Y (3) If not currently smoking, have you quit smoking in the last year? N Y (2) Recreational drugs? N Y (3)				
TOTAL				

Section 5: General Health History

Lifestyle	0	1	2	3
Frequency of exercise (days per week) 6-7, 3-5, 1-2, 0 (0) (1) (2) (3)				
Vegetarian or vegan N Y (2)				
Age >50 years N Y (3)				
Planning to have a baby in the next 3-6 months N Y (3)				
Pregnant or breastfeeding N Y (3)				
TOTAL				

References

D'Adamo, Dr. Peter. *Right for Your Type. New York, G.P. Putnam's Sons, 1996.*

Mallia, Dr J. *Concepts of Integrative Medicine. Sydney, NSW, Bookpal, 2012.*

Printed in the United States
By Bookmasters